egg

Lindsay & Patrick Mikanowski
Photographs by Grant Symon

Flammarion

contents

 separated yolk and white

EACH RECIPE BEARS ONE OF THE ABOVE SYMBOLS,
DEPENDING ON THE CATEGORIZATION SHOWN ON THIS
AND THE FACING PAGE.

Eggs, from largest to smallest: Ostrich (*Struthio camelus australis*); Ñandù (*Rhea americana*); Emu (*Dromaius novaehollandiae*), anthracite, laid by a 3-year old bird; Emu, gray, laid by a 2-year old bird; Emu, light gray, laid by a 1-year old bird; Mallard (*Anas platyrhynchos*); Chicken (*Gallus gallus*), brown; Chicken, white (the color of the shell is determined by the breed and diet of the hen); Bantam (*Gallus gallus*), Pheasant (*Phasianus colchicus*), ochre; Pheasant, light blue; Quail (*Coturnix coturnix*).

the difficulty of cooking with eggs. In these traditions, only whole eggs are used, either beaten or cooked in their shell. If at any point a yolk is pierced, no harm is done, since it will never need to be separated from the white. Eggs are unpredictable. Cracking one open may result in a burst yolk; the grudging egg sometimes refuses to be used in quite the way you want.

By their enduring presence in our kitchens, eggs have fostered in generations of cooks a special awareness of their unique characteristics and capricious behavior. From the Middle Ages on, many European traditions used yolks and whites separately. The whites would be used in marzipan or macaroons, while pâtés and Viennese pastries were brushed with egg yolk. But it was in classic French cooking that the independent culinary possibilities of the separate parts of the egg were developed fully. The creations that resulted from this experimentation have spread to the kitchens of the world, and their French names have passed unchanged into the gastronomic vocabulary of countless languages. *Soufflé, meringue, mousse, mayonnaise, omelette,* and *pâtisserie* are to be found on the menus of every continent.

Some basic moves have to be mastered before one can tackle these advanced dishes, however. The first task is to master the knack of breaking the shell and removing the contents without harming the yolk. The movement required is a single, sharp, but controlled tap, cracking the shell surface only. It can take a while before this movement comes right every time. Once the shell is cracked, the fingers firmly pull apart the two halves, taking care again not to break the yolk. As it falls from the open shell, the yolk may also break under the shock of hitting the bowl. A wise precaution is to slide it out of the shell and into the bowl using a side plate or saucer (see illustration, page 22).

The next fundamental stage consists of separating the yolk from the white. Everybody

should be able to perform this correctly. The risk of failure is just as high as when breaking the egg. The slightest golden streaks from a broken yolk will prevent an egg white from being whisked into a foam. And that yolk cannot be cleared up; you've lost a white, a yolk, and you're not even left with a nice-looking egg. The choice is limited: omelet or scrambled eggs. Such irritations can put you in a bad mood; your misgivings increase as you start over, and the likelihood of success drops still further. An egg separator can save you all this inconvenience or, failing that, a large-holed strainer will do as good a job (see page 22).

Whisking yolks while adding oil causes them to undergo a mysterious transformation into a smooth, light golden mayonnaise. In theory…. Everyone has a memory of a disastrous mayonnaise. Despite following the rules to the letter—starting with a little vinegar or mustard, taking the eggs out of the fridge an hour

Still life: Le *Menu de maigre* (Meager Fare), 1731, oil on canvas, by Jean-Baptiste Siméon Chardin (1699–1779). The pan in the middle of the picture would be perfect for making omelets. The long handle would allow it to be used on the fire.
2, 3. Using a professional egg topper to make a clean cut across the shell.
4. An egg separator. The yolk remains in the separator while the whites are collected in the bottom part.

before, beating the yolks with a drizzle of oil at the same temperature, you somehow end up with an oily mess. The more frenetically you try to salvage it, the more it remains obstinately indifferent to your efforts.

Just one or two such disappointing failures are enough to put most people off. But using an electric hand blender and a tallish container, just wider than the head of the blender, will practically guarantee that your mayonnaise comes together. It is not necessary for the eggs to be at room temperature. And if a mayonnaise is starting to fall apart, a little water added to the mixture can work miracles.

The same bewilderment can be caused by a soufflé. Use all the tips and tricks you like to guarantee that the mixture you put into the oven will rise to the heavens—sometimes it just comes out as a pot of shriveled custard. The egg whites were expertly beaten to stiff, snowy peaks and then lovingly folded into a smooth sauce of milk, egg yolks, and flour. How can it not have turned into a soufflé? What did you do to make this magical, fluffy cloud break its promise? Who hasn't paced expectantly in front of the oven door, fearing the worst? And when it comes out of the heat, what is to be done to stop it collapsing straight away? If all the un-runny omelets, rubbery brioches, and deformed sponge cakes to come out of an oven were laid end to end.... Eggs are at the root of so many disappointments and failures in the kitchen. Yet an understanding of the basic chemistry of eggs, and a readiness to combine this with the use of some specialized equipment, can keep at least these disasters out of a cook's catalogue of culinary flops.

hygiene and diet: walking on eggshells?

The egg, so popular fears would have it, has a dark side. Within that shell lurks a fifth column of bacteria and viruses, from salmonella to bird flu, just waiting to break out and get us. In reality, infection levels are very low, and cases of salmonella are relatively rare. In any case, the dangers are very easy to avoid. Always examine eggs before using them to check the shell is not cracked. Wash your hands with hot water and soap after touching eggshells. The shells should be thrown away immediately, not allowed to pile up on the work surface. Most importantly, eggs must be cooked before being eaten: salmonella bacteria are destroyed after a few minutes above a temperature of 140°F (60°C), and the H5N1 virus is killed at temperatures above 160°F (70°C). An egg cooked to 160°F will have a yolk that has just set and a white which is still very supple.
But how healthy are eggs? They are reputed to be very high in cholesterol. In fact, studies over the last ten years have shown that the amount of cholesterol in our bodies due to our diet is negligible: 80 percent of the cholesterol in the blood comes from the liver, where it is produced. One egg yolk does contain two-thirds of an adult's recommended daily allowance of cholesterol, but most of it is not absorbed by the body.[8] Eggs are, on the other hand, a first-class source of complete, high-quality protein. The yolks contain a number of vitamins and trace elements and are very easily digested. The white consists of protein and water, while the yolk also contains some fat, though this is mostly unsaturated.
Eggs are complex little coffers of unpredictability, unable to reveal their inner nature immediately. We can unravel this complexity by gaining a better understanding of the phenomena at work when cooking with eggs. How important is the freshness of the eggs we use? What are we looking for in an egg? If we want to make the most of its flavor, we have to know what that flavor is, and how freshness can affect that. We must understand some of the chemistry and physics behind the

"for best results, eggs must be extra-fresh

egg's protean capacity to transform itself under the effect of heat or emulsification. And what of its nutritive qualities? Are eggs receiving the attention they deserve as a health food?

freshness

The freshness of an egg can be established by candling: when held in front of a strong, focused light source, the state of the contents can be observed. A small air sac and an opaque white are good signs. Freshness is of prime importance when cooking successfully with eggs, not only for reasons of hygiene, but also taste and texture. A rotten egg will give off a characteristic smell of sulfur when broken—although by then it may be too late. If in doubt, crack each egg into an empty bowl before adding it to other ingredients. But long before they become rotten, older eggs can be unsuitable for certain dishes. Some knowledge of the different stages of freshness can help to avoid unpleasant surprises. Some tips for checking freshness are given on page 22.

Partridge Wyandottes brooding in the henhouse. The Wyandotte was developed in New York State at the end of the 19th century. These robust hens make decent layers and excellent mothers, while the heavy cockerel makes a good table bird.

The date on the packaging of store-bought eggs—when present and legible—is a good place to start. In the United States, a USDA shield and a grade of AA is an indicator of freshness, as well as the esthetic quality of the shell, white, and yolk. But it can be a good idea to take the time to check, especially when the success of a dish depends on the freshness of the egg. Eggs for boiling or omelets should be as fresh as possible, whereas meringues can be made—and in fact are better—with whites that have been separated and kept in the refrigerator for several days.

When flavor matters the most, eggs must be *extra*-fresh. This means that no more than twenty-four hours must have gone by between laying and reaching the store. Extra-fresh eggs have become harder for most people to find these days, as the smaller farmyards in rural areas have dwindled and urban populations have mushroomed. All too often, the production site is a long way from the point of sale, and the flavor of the eggs peaks while they are still in transport. On the farm, a freshly laid egg might only wait for twelve hours before being eaten. But for the flavor to be at its very best, the extra-fresh egg must come from a free-range hen fed on a varied, grain-rich diet. That ultimate flavor is something close to the taste of handmade unsalted dairy butter. So if you're after the perfect soft-boiled egg, the ideal omelet, or supreme scrambled eggs, do your best to find extra-fresh eggs. For the best ways of cooking them, see unboiled eggs, below.

When "very" fresh eggs are the best we can hope for, how can we spot the freshest ones? Other than candling, another reliable way to judge freshness is by careful observation. The yolk, the white, and the shell all give visual clues. The shell should be velvety in texture, and have a slight glow to it. When a very fresh egg is cracked onto a plate, the yolk will be well rounded and firm, offering resistance when prodded gently. The surrounding white will be thick, and have a light yellow hue with a hint of green. There will be a small amount of fluid at the outer edge. The less fresh the egg, the flatter the yolk, and the more liquid and colorless the white.

A very fresh egg feels heavy in the hand. This is because almost all the space inside the shell is taken up with egg, rather than air. The air cell inside the shell starts off very tiny, measuring just over 1/8 inch (4 mm) in a very fresh egg, and reaching about 1/4 inch (6 mm) as gasses are exchanged through the shell. So the lighter, or less dense, an egg is, the less fresh it is. To check this, simply fill a large glass with water and place the egg in it. If it lies flat on the bottom, it is very fresh. If it floats halfway up, it is not so fresh, and if it floats above the surface it is not fresh at all, and should be thrown away (see illustration page 23).

The way eggs are stored is also of paramount importance to keep them in best condition. The shell, to begin with, should not be washed until the last moment, if at all. The outer layer of the shell is covered with a protective film, which deteriorates on contact with soap and water. Refrigeration has done a lot to prolong the freshness of eggs. If not kept at the bottom of the refrigerator, they should be kept out of draughts, but in a well-aerated place, at a temperature below 52°F (12°C). They should also be kept away from sources of light. As long as these guidelines are followed and there is no interruption in the cold chain, keeping very fresh eggs in the refrigerator for up to two weeks poses no problem from a food hygiene point of view.

the unboiled egg

Chemistry has a vital role to play in the science of gastronomy. It allows us to understand the transformations that foodstuffs undergo when exposed to heat, or combined with fat, or when acidic or alkaline solutions are added. The French chemist, Hervé This, is a specialist in "molecular gastronomy" at the Collège de France. One of his areas of study has been the reaction of egg proteins to different levels of heat.

According to his research, at 149°F (65°C) precisely the white will coagulate without getting tough, while the yolk remains smooth and fluid. When you have gone to the trouble of obtaining the freshest eggs possible, cooking them at this temperature will get the best out of them. The equivalent of a boiled

" chemistry has a vital role to play

in the science of gastronomy "

1. Opening an egg cooked at 149°F (65°C).
2. The white and yolk cooked at 149°F (65°C).
3. At 149°F (65°C), the yolk is warm and liquid.
4. When cooked at 155°F (68°C) the white is more solid.
5. At 155°F (68°C) the yolk is thicker.

three-minute or five-minute egg cooked in this way—although it will take much longer than three or five minutes, and will never be boiled—is far superior in flavor and structure. The process is also very forgiving of the quality of the egg; even an ordinary egg takes on an incomparable taste and texture. The warm yolk turns an intense golden color, with a creamy yet runny texture, and a rounded, sweet taste of butter. The surrounding white is slightly warmer, and has no taste; it sets without going hard, adding nothing more than a contrast in texture. In structure it is like an opaque white jelly, a long way from the rubbery elasticity of eggs boiled in water. The white is also free of that whiff of sulfur produced when an egg is cooked at a high temperature; at 149°F the odor is perfectly neutral.

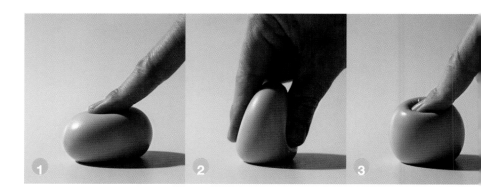

According to Hervé This, baking in the oven is the easiest way of maintaining the correct temperature. The proteins in the yolk begin to coagulate at 155°F (68°C), those in the white at 144°F (62°C). An egg weighing about 2 ½ oz (70 g) will need at least two hours in the oven at 149°F (65°C) to be cooked evenly. As long as the temperature remains within the range 144°F to 155°F (62°C to 68°C), the degree of doneness will not change a great deal over the space of a few hours. So before leaving in the morning you can put some eggs in to cook—in an egg box for example—and by the time you take them out in the evening, the yolks will still be runny and the whites just set. You will need to check the accuracy of your oven's thermostat with a thermometer: unfortunately, domestic ovens are often unreliable in that respect. A thermometer is definitely needed if you want to cook the eggs this way in a pan of water.

sunny side up

Some of the greatest French chefs over the last century have focused their attention on the fried egg. In the search for a white that is only just solidified, and a creamy smooth yolk which runs onto the plate when pierced, chefs like Fernand Point, Bernard Loiseau, and Alain Passard (see page 82) have applied the principles described above with an empirical approach, using mainly visual clues. Fernand Point (1897–1955) used to enjoy defeating his trainee chefs by asking them to make a fried egg. When the aspiring candidates failed, as he knew they would, he would benignly show them how it was done. A little fresh butter went into a skillet, and was melted silently over a very low heat, without sizzling or frothing, until it covered the bottom of the pan. Point then slid the egg into the pan from a small saucer, and cooked it until the white was creamy and the yolk hot but still runny. He would transfer the egg onto a warmed plate and season it with salt and pepper, then pour on melted butter prepared earlier in a separate pan.

In contrast to Point's classical love of butter, the nouvelle cuisine of Bernard Loiseau (1951–2003) had a lighter touch. But even he started with butter, putting a very small amount in a saucer over a small pan of boiling water. Once the butter had melted, he cooked the egg in the saucer, taking care to avoid all direct contact with the strong heat from the boiling water. He advised separating the yolk and white before cooking, intuitively allowing for the different coagulation temperatures.

1, 2 and 3: When soaked in vinegar for a few days, the calcium carbonate in the shell dissolves, and it becomes completely soft. If hardboiled before soaking, the egg will bounce when dropped.

the expert omelet

Rudolph Stanish (1913–), expert American omeleteer, has cooked for many famous names including John F. Kennedy and Princess Diana. He places a great deal of importance on the quality of the pan. First, it should be an appropriate size for the number of eggs used. It is difficult to make a good omelet with a large number of eggs, both for reasons of manageability—the weight of the pan, the inconvenience of whisking a large number of eggs—and the necessity of keeping the omelet relatively thin. The following instructions are for an omelet with four eggs, each weighing about 2 ½ oz (70 g), and a pan with a bottom diameter of 7 inches (15–17 mm). It can be made of cast iron, stainless steel, or aluminum, but must always be heavy, with a thick base and sides, and must only be used for making omelets. Before it is used for the first time, it must be seasoned: melt a small amount of oil or butter (according to taste) in the new pan and scour the base and sides with a little salt and kitchen paper.

Thereafter, the omelet pan is never to be washed again, just wiped clean with kitchen paper, rubbing out any bits of stuck-on egg with a little salt if necessary. The amount of butter or oil used for the first few omelets should be generous, but the more the pan is used the better it gets, and the less fat it will need to cook without sticking. If the pan is made of aluminum, the inside should be rubbed to a shine with wire wool before being seasoned.

The four eggs must be as fresh as possible. Break them into a bowl and beat them, but not so much that the mixture becomes homogenous and thin. When the whisk is lifted the egg should form shiny, stretchy, slightly sticky ribbons. Add two large spoonfuls of water or beer, along with a good pinch of salt, a few drops of Tabasco sauce and a little pepper, mixing gently all the while. The pan should be impeccably clean (that is, free from any trace of food) every time it is used. Heat the pan until hot enough to make drops of water spit, jump, and disappear immediately.

Melt ½ stick (50 g) of butter into the pan and run it around the bottom. A soon as the butter stops frothing, add the egg mixture. Lift the egg as it cooks with circular, horizontal movements of the fork, forming layers, while shaking the pan with the other hand. Quickly pull the edges away from the side of the skillet as they start to catch, and tip the mixture into the gap, until the omelet is loosely set.
At this stage, the surface of the omelet is still loose, uneven, and shiny. Remove from the heat and turn your hand round to hold the pan with fingers upward, thumb outward. Tipping the pan at 45°, with your hand at the top of the slope, roll the omelet down the pan with the fork, starting near the handle. When you reach the other side, slide the omelet straight onto a warm plate. Eggs will continue to cook in a hot pan even when off the heat, so this has to be done quickly. Two important tips: use unsalted butter and don't let it color when melting. And white pepper is much more appetizing: even finely ground black pepper can give the impression that the omelet has had volcanic sand kicked onto it.

If the other ingredients are warm (diced bacon, mushrooms, sautéed potatoes, asparagus tips), add them just before pouring the eggs into the pan. If the egg mixture is to be flavored, for example with truffle shavings or herbs, they should be mixed with the beaten egg before adding water and the mixture left for a quarter of an hour before cooking, to let the flavors infuse. Any sauce to be added (tomato, onion compote) must be prepared in advance and kept warm. Just before the omelet is rolled, spoon or pour the sauce onto the third of the omelet furthest away from the pan handle.

scrambled eggs decoded

For a better understanding of scrambled eggs, let us turn to another American. M.F.K. Fisher (1908–1992) was a prolific writer on food and the art of living, and translated Brillat-Savarin's classic, *The Physiology of Taste.*

Her approach to scrambling eggs requires a deal of patience: she recommends half an hour over a very low but direct heat, stirring constantly. The low-risk alternative is to use a bain-marie: cook the eggs in a small four-inch pan, sitting this pan in a larger one containing boiling water. Only the most intrepid cook will attempt scrambled eggs without the use of this safety net. The indirect heat causes the proteins to coagulate more gently, allowing the egg to retain a creamy texture.

As with the omelet, the mixture for scrambled eggs is not beaten for long. Around ten seconds is enough: it should remain thick. Ali Bab advocated straining the eggs through a sieve to remove the membranes and other particles, but not beating them. For five people you will need ten eggs, ½ cup (125 g) butter, ½ cup (125 g) cream (warmed in the microwave), and a little salt and white pepper. Add a little of the butter to the inner pan of the bain-marie and, once it has melted, add the eggs and stir continuously. As soon as the mixture begins to thicken, remove from the heat and incorporate the rest of the butter in small pieces, the warm cream, and season with salt and pepper. The scrambled eggs should be served at once, heaped onto buttered toast on warm plates. A tasty alternative can be made by sweating a finely chopped onion in butter before adding the eggs, and flavoring the mixture with a teaspoon of very fresh curry powder, and as much finely chopped parsley as you please.

stress-free soufflé

A soufflé can be made with an equal number of whites and yolks, but the addition of one or two extra whites will help to keep luck on your side. Use very fresh eggs. The secret of a soufflé is to preheat the oven properly, not to have it on too high a heat, and to minimize the time and distance between taking the soufflé out of the oven and serving it. Dinner guests must come to the table before the soufflé does. Preheat the oven to 400°F (200°C) for at least twenty minutes. Use as many eggs as there are people. Separate the eggs, beat the yolks and keep to one side. Prepare a soufflé dish by buttering the inside and coating it with breadcrumbs: this helps the soufflé to rise. A piece of baking parchment wrapped around the top of the dish, also buttered and sprinkled with breadcrumbs, will accentuate the rising effect. The paper should be removed with a knife before serving.

Start by preparing a béchamel sauce. Stir together ½ stick (50 g) butter and a tablespoonful of flour over a low heat. Slowly add 1 cup (250 g) of cream, stirring into the roux only as it starts to boil, to avoid lumps. The sauce should be smooth and shiny. If it is too thick, add cream, always warming it before mixing in. The consistency to aim for is that of light cream. Add nutmeg, salt, and pepper for seasoning. Take the pan off the heat and stir in around 2 ½ cups (200–300 g) of grated cheese, for example Gruyère or Parmesan. Then mix in the whisked yolks, which should be pale yellow in color. Beat the whites until very firm. Add them to the mixture a portion at a time, bringing the sauce over the foam in light layers so as not to flatten it, using a large wooden spoon. Pour the mixture very gently into the soufflé dish, and put in the oven for around forty minutes.

When it comes to cooking with eggs, whatever the dish, both the eggs and the cook have everything to gain from carrying out the preparation in a spirit of calm detachment.

Jean-François Piège's perfect soufflé.

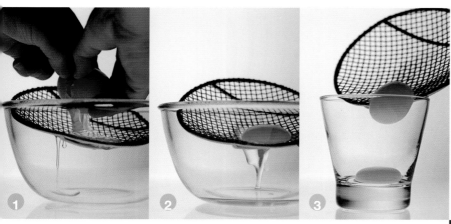

how to separate an egg

If you are not feeling too clever with your hands, simply break the egg into a sieve or a Chinese spider **(1)**. The white falls through into the receptacle **(2)** while the yolk remains on the spider, and can be slid into a glass **(3)**.

how to beat egg whites

For the firmest, fluffiest egg whites, make sure the mixing bowl is cold and all utensils are scrupulously clean. Start beating slowly to break up the structure of the whites, then add a pinch of salt and gradually whisk faster. An electric whisk is easier, and faster. Beaten egg whites will not keep, so always prepare them at the last minute.

how to add egg whites

When adding beaten whites to any preparation, start by folding in just one or two tablespoonfuls of whites to loosen the mixture. Then add the remaining whites in one go, turning them in with a lifting motion using a wooden spoon.

how to recognize fresh eggs

Before eggs were date-stamped, one traditional method of choosing the freshest eggs for boiling was to float them. Place an egg in a glass of water; if it is fresh,

Six degrees of separation of the yolk from the white.

tips

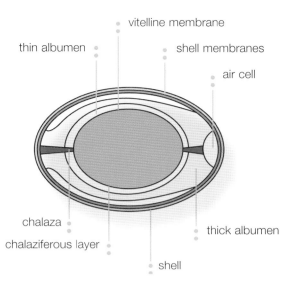

vitelline membrane
thin albumen
shell membranes
air cell
chalaza
chalaziferous layer
thick albumen
shell

it will sink **(1)**. An egg over five days old contains more air, and will float. If an egg floats above the surface, throw it away **(2)**.

An average egg weighs about two ounces (60 g), with a variation of ½ oz (15 g) either way. It consists of: a water and gas permeable shell, made mostly of calcium carbonate, constituting around 11 percent of the weight of the egg;tough, fibrous shell membranes, made of the same material as hair and feathers; the white, which is composed
of several layers of thick and thin albumen (10 percent proteins in water), and the rope-like chalazae, which hold the yolk in the center of the egg; the yolk, enclosed in the clear vitelline membrane, which is only about half water, the other half being proteins, vitamins, minerals, and

fat, as well as lecithin, which acts as an emulsifier; an air cell, which forms as the egg's contents cool and contract after laying.

how to tell a hard-boiled egg from a raw egg

In the refrigerator, all eggs look the same. How can you tell whether an egg has been hard-boiled or is still raw?
One solution is to set the egg spinning on a smooth surface. A hard-boiled egg will spin more easily. Once it is spinning, stop it very briefly with your forefinger. If it continues to turn when your finger is removed, the egg is raw: the liquid contents continue to move inside after the shell has stopped.
Another solution is to add a few drops of food dye to the water whenever you boil eggs. The darker color of the hard-boiled eggs will allow you to spot them immediately in the refrigerator among the paler, raw eggs.
A third method of finding out whether an egg is raw or hard-boiled, for those who really lack patience: drop one on the floor!

40 crack

ing dishes

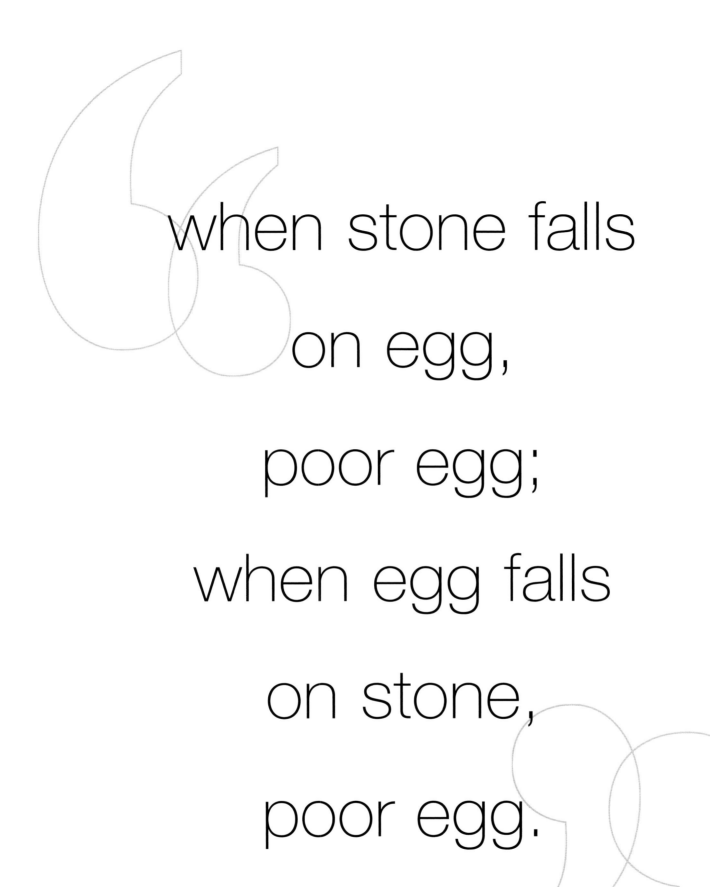

"when stone falls

on egg,

poor egg;

when egg falls

on stone,

poor egg."

paul pairet
quoting a Chinese proverb

JADE ON 36 (PUDONG SHANGRI-LA HOTEL), SHANGHAI, CHINA

goose egg smoked in China tea

serves 4

4 goose eggs

lapsang souchong salt
4 tablespoons (10 g) lapsang
  souchong
½ cup (100 g) olive oil
1 tablespoon sugar
1 pinch citric acid (available
  from specialized outlets)
1 tablespoon Sel de Guérande
  (unrefined sea salt)
1 tablespoon coarsely ground
  black pepper

Chinese smoking mixture
3 tablespoons jasmine rice
4 tablespoons (10 g) jasmine tea
2 tablespoons sugar
1 star anise, crushed
¼ cinnamon stick, crushed

Alternative to lapsang
souchong salt:
soy sauce
Szechwan pepper

1 LAPSANG SOUCHONG SALT
Deep-fry the tea in olive oil until crunchy.
Add other ingredients and cook for an additional
minute. Drain on paper towels.

2 CHINESE SMOKING MIXTURE
Mix together the rice, tea, sugar, and crushed
spices.

3
Wash and dry the eggs. Place the eggs, standing
on their points, in an airtight container with the
smoking mixture. Stands can be made from
cardboard egg-box sections. Close the container
and set aside in the refrigerator for at least
24 hours.

4 SMOKING
Line the bottom of a steamer pot with aluminum
foil. Spread the smoking mixture to a thickness of
about ¼ inch (5 mm). Line the rim of the pot with
three layers of foil to create a seal with the upper
part of the steamer. Place the cold eggs on their
stands in the steamer basket. Now line the rim of
the top part of the steamer with foil, put the lid on
and fold the foil over to create a hermetic seal.
Place over high heat for one to two minutes. As
soon as smoke appears, remove from heat. Set
aside unopened at room temperature for at least
four hours; the smoking process continues even
when cold.

PRESERVATION
The eggs can be kept at this stage for several days
in a properly airtight container in the refrigerator. But
they are never better than when cooked directly
after smoking.

5
Boil the eggs for two or three minutes, or steam
for ten minutes. Serve immediately with the
lapsang souchong salt, or with soy sauce
and Szechwan pepper.

RECOMMENDED DRINK TAIWANESE
LAPSANG SOUCHONG TEA

"
the egg,
in its divine
perfection,
embodies
all the
causes
and effects

of karma…
yet for
those who
brave it,
it is
delicious.
"

éric ripert

LE BERNARDIN, NEW YORK

osetra caviar in carbonara nest

a quail's egg

1 pound (500 g) tagliatelle
¼ cup (30 g) very finely diced
  smoked ham
1 tablespoon crushed
  black pepper
¼ (30 g) stick butter
1 cup (250 ml) crème fraîche
⅓ cup (15 g) finely chopped chives
3 tablespoons freshly grated
  Parmesan
4 quail's eggs
4 ¼ ounces (120 g) osetra caviar
unrefined sea salt and black
  pepper, for grinding

1
Cook the tagliatelle until al dente, drain, and
set aside.

2
Brown the finely diced ham in a large sauté pan.

3
Season with black pepper and cook for an
additional minute.

4
Remove from heat and add crème fraîche, butter,
chives, and Parmesan. Combine and add seasoning
to taste.

5
Share out the tagliatelle into four soup plates,
making a nest in each.

6
Place a quail yolk in each nest, cover with caviar,
and serve immediately.

RECOMMENDED WINE WHITE PRIORAT,
COMA BLANCA 1999, MAS D'EN GIL

"
he who eats
the egg does
not know
if the chicken
has a sore
backside.
"

caviar "egg roll"

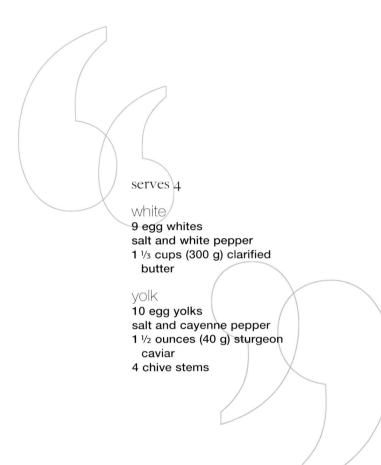

serves 4

white
9 egg whites
salt and white pepper
1 ⅓ cups (300 g) clarified
   butter

yolk
10 egg yolks
salt and cayenne pepper
1 ½ ounces (40 g) sturgeon
   caviar
4 chive stems

1 WHITE
Season the egg whites with salt and white pepper. Beat with an electric whisk for 30 seconds, strain, and allow to rest for five minutes. Pour into a flexible container.

2
Heat the clarified butter to 165°F (75°C) in a medium-sized pan. Remove from heat and drizzle whites into the pan until the bottom is entirely covered. Place the pan back on the heat for 15 seconds, then allow to rest for five minutes until the whites are puffy and firm.

3
Use a spatula to lift the sheet of whites out of the pan in two or three pieces. Place on a paper towel and season with salt. When the fat has been absorbed, cut into strips one inch by four (2.5 by 10 cm), and set aside.

1 YOLK
Beat the yolks with the salt and Cayenne pepper until smooth.

2
Pour the yolks into a fairly rigid plastic food bag measuring 2 x 10 inches (5 x 25 cm) and knot the end. Leave to rest for two to three hours until the bubbles rise to the surface.

3
Prepare a bain-marie at 68°C (155°F) and cook the bag, still upright, for two hours. Set aside in the refrigerator for at least two hours.

4
Cut the bag open and remove the set yolk.

1 DRESSING
Cut the yolk cylinder into one-inch (2.5-cm) lengths and roll each piece up in an egg-white strip. Leave at room temperature for 15 to 20 minutes.

2
Top each "egg roll" with a teaspoonful of American sturgeon caviar and decorate with a chive.

RECOMMENDED WINE WHITE HERMITAGE BLANC 1999, JEAN-LOUIS CHAVE

" if you over-milk the cow, you'll kill the goose that lays the golden egg. "

thomas keller
quoting henri jeanson

PER SE, NEW YORK

truffle-pickled hen eggs with a truffle marmalade friand

1
Dissolve the sugar in a mixture of truffle juice and champagne vinegar. This will be the marinade.

2
Hard-boil the eggs and allow to cool. Peel and place in the marinade for at least 24 hours but no longer than 72 hours. Keep the liquid.

3
Cut the eggs in half lengthwise, and remove and keep the yolks.

4
Fill the cavities in the whites with the marinade, and leave in the refrigerator to soak in.

5
Pass the yolks through a fine sieve. Gently mix with the whipped crème fraîche and season with salt and truffle oil.

6
Spoon this filling into a piping bag with a fluted nozzle.

7
Reduce the remaining marinade.

serves 6
half an egg per person

3 eggs
1 cup (200 g) sugar
⅔ cup (150 g) truffle juice
½ cup (100 g) champagne vinegar
1 ¼ cups (150 g) whipped crème fraîche
salt
truffle oil

truffle marmalade (1 cup)
1 tablespoon butter
⅓ cup (65 g) chopped shallots
2 ounces (65 g) chopped truffles
1 tablespoon sugar
1 ½ cups (375 ml) port
⅓ cup (75 g) reduced veal bouillon
salt and pepper

friands
1 cup (135 g) wheat flour
¾ cup (85 g) pastry flour (type 45)
1 tablespoon sugar
1 small pinch salt
1 pinch baking soda
1 ½ tablespoons very cold water
2 teaspoons white wine vinegar
1 cup (100 g) butter, in cold pieces
2 ½ tablespoons (35 g) lard, in cold pieces
chopped truffle to garnish

1 TRUFFLE MARMALADE

Sweat the shallots in butter over low heat until soft.
Add the chopped truffles and cook for five minutes until
strong aromas are released.

2

Add the sugar and caramelize lightly, then add the port
and reduce to a syrupy consistency.

3

Add the bouillon, season, and allow to cool.

1 TRUFFLE MARMALADE FRIANDS

Mix together the flours, sugar, salt, and baking soda.

2

Mix the water and the vinegar separately.

3

Push the butter and lard into the flour mixture with a
scraper, to form a lumpy mixture.

4

Stir in the liquid with a fork to bring the dough together.

5

Work the dough delicately into a compact ball. Cover
with plastic wrap and refrigerate.

1 SHAPING THE FRIANDS

Roll out the cold dough into thin, translucent sheets.

2

Cut pieces for the top and bottom layers with a pastry-
cutter. Using a fork, mark each top piece with three
parallel lines.

3

Spread half a teaspoon of truffle marmalade on the
bottom piece as a filling, add the top piece, and seal
the edges.

4

Cut again to leave a clean rectangle. Freeze the friands.
Cook directly from frozen in the oven at 350°F (180°C)
for five to seven minutes.

FINISHING

With marinade, sketch out a circle in the middle of the
plate. Place a half egg in the centre. Pipe a spiral of yolk
filling onto the egg. Serve with a truffle marmalade friand
topped with pieces of chopped truffle.

RECOMMENDED WINE SERCIAL MADEIRA
1978, BARBEITO

"it may be the cock
it is the hen that

that crows, but lays the eggs.

terence and vicki conran
quoting margaret thatcher

ZINC BAR AND GRILL, LONDON

serves 4

clarified jellied chicken bouillon (for the gelée)
½ cup (25 g) dried ceps
2 pounds (1 kg) chicken wings
1 leek
1 carrot
1 onion
1 sprig thyme
1 bay leaf
4 tablespoons white wine
2 cups (500 ml) mineral water

clarification
1 chicken breast
1 egg white
salt and pepper

œufs en gelée
8 eggs
2 cups (50 cl) clarified jellied chicken bouillon
2 sprigs fresh tarragon, quickly blanched
8 small dishes

1 CLARIFIED JELLIED BOUILLON
Pre-heat the oven to 400°F (200°C). Soak the ceps in a cup of warm water.

2
Chop the chicken wings, the leek, and the carrot, and cut the onion in half. Place everything in a roasting pan and roast for ten minutes, or until the meat and the onion have begun to brown.

3
Transfer to a casserole and add the ceps with their soaking juice, the thyme, and the bay leaf. Turn the oven down to 300°F (150°C). Deglaze the roasting pan with the white wine, add the juices to the casserole, then add the water. The pieces of wing should be covered. Cover and cook on low heat for 20 minutes, then in the oven for 40 minutes.

4
Strain the bouillon into a mixing bowl, pressing the juices out of the wings and vegetables. Leave to cool. Add salt and pepper.

This bouillon can be kept for one week in the refrigerator if boiled every two days.

1 CLARIFICATION
Bring the chicken bouillon to simmer, and add the chopped breast meat and the egg white. Whisk gently.

2
Adjust the heat to just below a boil and leave to simmer for 30 minutes. The white skin that forms at the surface contains all the impurities: remove it with a skimmer, leaving the clarified bouillon.

3
Filter the bouillon through a muslin-lined sieve, to remove the egg white and chopped chicken. Leave to cool, and refrigerate. The gelée is ready.

1 ŒUFS EN GELÉE
Warm some clarified bouillon and pour a tablespoonful into each dish. Add a few tarragon leaves. Refrigerate until the bouillon jellifies.

2
Boil some water in a large high-sided frying pan, remove from heat, and delicately break the eggs into the water. Cover and leave for three minutes. The eggs are done when the whites are firm and the yolks still soft.

3
Lift the eggs out one by one with a slotted spoon and place them on kitchen paper on a plate. Refrigerate to make the eggs firmer. When all the eggs have been poached, drained, and firmed, place them one by one in the dishes.

4
Use a spoon to cover the eggs with another layer of bouillon, which will now have cooled to a more syrupy consistency. Cover the molds with plastic film and refrigerate.

RECOMMENDED WINE WHITE CÔTE DE BEAUNE, CHASSAGNE-MONTRACHET 2001, DOMAINE RAMONET

œufs en gelée

" it's like the chicken and the egg: which came first? "

serves 4

8 large eggs
2 sheets phyllo pastry
¼ cup (60 ml) olive oil
2 strips dry-cured ham
¾ cup (200 ml) red beet juice
½ cup (100 ml) wine vinegar
10 ounces (300 g) celeriac

¾ cup (200 ml) water
¾ cup (200 ml) milk
4 cloves garlic
2 bay leaves
1 ½ ounces (40 g) black truffles
¼ stick (30 g) butter, for
  greasing the ramekins
unrefined sea salt
freshly ground pepper

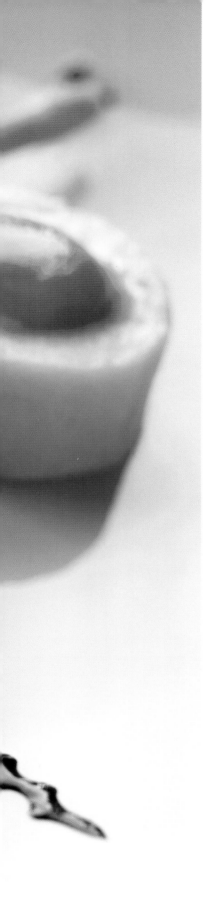

celeriac and truffle egg duet

1

Cut each sheet of phyllo in half and brush with olive oil. Lay a strip of ham on each piece and roll into a fine tube. Place the sticks on a baking tray and cook for three minutes at 425°F (220°C). Set aside.

2

Reduce the beet juice with the vinegar to make a sharp, syrupy "gastrique."* Set aside.

3

Peel the celeriac with a knife and cut into cubes. Cook with the water, milk, garlic, and bay leaves for 20 minutes, then strain. Add a little of the cooking liquid back in, and liquidize. Set aside.

4

Separate the eggs, taking care not to pierce the yolks. Divide the whites into two bowls. Add the chopped truffle to one and the pureed celeriac to the other. Cook equal amounts of the two mixtures in eight small buttered ramekins for six minutes. Add an egg yolk to the center of each ramekin and cook for a further five minutes.

5

Remove the ramekins from the oven, turn out the eggs, and arrange one celeriac and one truffle egg on each plate.

Dress the plate with the crunchy stick and lines of beet gastrique. Sprinkle a few grains of salt and coarsely ground pepper on the yolks.

RECOMMENDED WINE WHITE PESSAC-LÉOGNAN, DOMAINE DE CHEVALIER 2002

* see glossary, page 190

"when you crack open an egg you do not necessarily break its secret; but to watch its yolk spreading is to experience all its sensuality."

judith baumann

LA PINTE DES MOSSETTES, LA VALSAINTE, SWITZERLAND

1 YOLK

Deseed and season the sweet pepper. Preserve it in olive oil it at 275°F (90°C) for three hours, turning every hour.

Scramble the eggs and mix in the ricotta and cream. Season. Blanch the spinach in salted water and dry well. Distribute the scrambled egg in the bottom of four yolk molds. Add a layer of spinach. Peel the pepper and cut out four 1 ½-inch (4-cm) discs with a pastry cutter. Add a disc to each mold. Leave for two hours in the refrigerator with a weight on top, to compress the layers. Peel the bird pepper and cut into fine strips.

2 TARRAGON JELLY

Make a tarragon infusion with the veal bouillon. Leave covered until cool, then remove the tarragon. Stir in the agar and cook for two to three minutes. Season and pour onto plates. Leave to set.

3 CURL

Melt the chocolate in a bain-marie or equivalent at 125°F (52°C). Work it on a marble slab with a palette knife until cooled to 80°F (27°C), then warm up again to 88°F (31°C). Spread a layer of chocolate onto the slab and allow to cool very slightly. Peel off four wide, thin curls with the side of the palette knife.

4 GARNISH

Deep-fry the tarragon in oil at 265°F (130°C). Dry on kitchen paper and salt lightly.

5 WHITE

Whisk the egg whites with the tea and salt. Using two spoons, form four medium-sized quenelles.

6 WRAPPER

Remove the yolks from the molds and place the strips of bird pepper on their base. Warm them in a steamer then wrap each yolk in its slice of Lardo d'Arnad. Place the wrapped yolks under the grill for a few moments until the lardo turns transparent. Poach and drain the egg-white quenelles. Arrange one quenelle and one yolk on the jelly bed of each plate. Finish off the plate by tucking the fried tarragon in the end of the quenelle, and resting a chocolate curl across it.

RECOMMENDED WINE WHITE CÔTES DU RHÔNE, MARSANNE BLANCHE 2004, BERNARD CAVÉ

serves 4

yolk
2 eggs
1 sweet pepper
1 tablespoon olive oil
1 ½ tablespoons ricotta
2 tablespoons heavy cream
1 large spinach leaf
1 bird pepper
salt and pepper
egg-yolk-shaped Flexipan molds,
   1 ½ inches (4 cm) in diameter.

tarragon jelly
¾ cup (200 ml) veal bouillon
2 sprigs tarragon
½ teaspoon agar
salt and pepper

curl
1 ½ ounces (40 g) chocolate,
   85% cocoa solids

garnish
4 attractive tarragon sprigs
groundnut oil
salt

white
3 egg whites
1 teaspoon matcha tea
salt

wrapper
4 thin slices Lardo d'Arnad
   (or Lardo di Colonnata),
   2 ½ inches (6 cm) square

egg, sweet pepper, chocolate, and matcha tea with tarragon jelly

jean-pierre biffi

POTEL & CHABOT, PARIS

"the white hen pecks for food, or flies and does without; little does she care of what tomorrow may bring for her egg."

upright eggs

serves 4

3 small beets

egg
**5 eggs
(1 in case of breakage)**

sauce
**¾ cup (175 g) shallots
1 ½ cups (100 g) mushrooms
¼ stick (25 g) butter
½ cup (10 cl) port
1 bottle (75 cl) Mercurey red wine
1 ½ sugar cubes
salt and pepper**

garnish
**a few very thin slices hazelnut
  and raisin bread (cut with
  a meat-slicer if possible)
1 ⅔ cups (250 g) fresh peas
1 cup (150 g) shelled broad beans
1 ½ cups (100 g) button
  mushrooms
15 baby carrots**

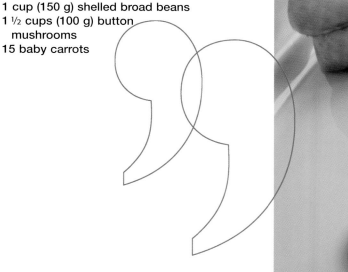

1 BEETS—THE DAY BEFORE

Wrap two of the beets in aluminum foil. Bake at
325°F (160°C) for 40 minutes to an hour,
depending on size. Peel and reduce to a fine purée
in a food processor.

2 EGGS—THE DAY BEFORE

Soft-boil the eggs for five minutes, shell, and place
in the beet purée. Set aside in the refrigerator until
the next day.

3 SAUCE AND GARNISH

The day you are serving the dish, chop the shallots,
the remaining raw beet, and the mushrooms, and
sweat in butter. Deglaze with port and reduce until
almost dry. Add the red wine and sugar and leave
to reduce by half. Thicken with beet purée. Strain
and season with salt, pepper, and a knob of butter.

4

Crisp up the bread in the oven at 300°F (150°C).
Briefly cook the vegetables in water, keeping them
crunchy.

5

Heat the eggs for two minutes in their sauce, then
garnish as shown.

RECOMMENDED WINE RED BURGUNDY,
MERCUREY, CLOS DES MYGLANDS 2001

meurette with beet

" there's white, there's yellow,

cédric béchade

PLAZA ATHÉNÉE, PARIS

there's a whole palette in an egg!

egg in a light gelée with piperade vinaigrette and onion jus soldiers

serves 4

1 smoked eel

onion jus soldiers
4 slices good handmade bread
3 white onions
½ cup (100 g) butter
1 ¼ cups (300 ml) white wine
2 pinches salt
2 pinches sugar

piperade vinaigrette
2 red peppers
olive oil

4 fresh piquillo peppers
2 white onions
2 tomatoes
¾ cup (200 ml) tomato concentrate
1 ¼ cups (300 ml) tomato juice
2 cloves garlic
2 cups (500 ml) white wine
¾ cup (200 ml) white bouillon
10 parsley stalks

sweet pepper gelée
4 extra-fresh eggs
6 green bull's horn peppers
1 clove garlic

powdered Espelette* pepper
2 sheets gelatine
salt

egg whites
3 ½ ounces (100 g) celeriac
7 ounces (200 g) fennel
2 onions
1 cup (250 ml) light cream
4 sheets gelatine

finishing
2 cups (500 ml) Barolo wine vinegar
olive oil

1 ONION JUS SOLDIERS

Cut the bread into strips. Peel and coarsely chop the onions. Melt the butter and heat until it begins to brown and give off a nutty aroma (*beurre noisette*). Brown the onions, then add two pinches of salt and two pinches of sugar.

2

Cover the pan and continue to cook for three minutes until caramelized. Deglaze with the white wine and add water to cover the onions by half an inch.

3

Cook down until the onions are exposed, then strain off the jus. Keep the onions for the piperade.

4

Sprinkle the soldiers with the onion jus and place in the oven until golden and crunchy.

1 PIPERADE VINAIGRETTE

Wash and deseed the red peppers. Remove all the white parts and the membrane from the inside.

2

Chop the onions, red peppers, and the piquillos. Cut the tomatoes into large pieces.

3

Heat a casserole and add the onions, tomato concentrate, peppers, and the onions from the jus. Brown and add the tomato juice. Simmer until caramelized.

4

Add the fresh tomatoes and garlic cloves, and deglaze with white wine.

5

Reduce by half and add the white bouillon and the parsley. Cook, covered, in a slow oven 250°F (120°C) for two hours.

6

Press through a sieve.

1 SWEET PEPPER GELÉE

Wash and deseed the bull's horn peppers, and remove the white parts and the inner membrane. Slice two of the peppers, and liquidize three others in a juicer. Brown the sliced peppers in a sauté pan and add the juiced peppers.

2

Add the garlic clove and cook for another five minutes.

3

Press through a sieve and season with salt and Espelette pepper.

4

Add the gelatine.

5

Separate the eggs. Cook the yolks in the oven for 15 minutes at 150°F (65°C). Reserve the whites.

6

Place each yolk in a pastry ring and pour the gelée round it, without covering the top. Set aside in the refrigerator.

7

Cut the remaining pepper into diamond shapes and toss in olive oil. Season.

1 EGG WHITES

Peel the celeriac and cut into even pieces. Wash and cut up the fennel, and peel and coarsely chop the onions.

2

Sweat the vegetables without browning. Add the cream and cook until the vegetables are done. Liquidize and add the gelatine. Set aside in a cool place.

3

Beat the egg whites and incorporate the vegetable mixture. Mold in a large pastry ring.

FINISHING

Season the piperade sauce with Barolo wine vinegar and whisk with olive oil. Center the white on the plate and place the jellied yolk in the middle of it. Skin the eel and break into segments. Intersperse the pepper diamonds with pieces of eel. Place a soldier on the side.

RECOMMENDED WINE PACHERENC, CUVÉE FRIMAIRE 2000, ALAIN BRUMONT

* see glossary, page 190

"the past
is a
broken egg,
the future
a hatched
egg."

alberto herráiz
quoting paul éluard

LE FOGON, PARIS

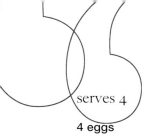

serves 4

4 eggs

preserved peppers
8 fresh piquillo peppers
2 tablespoons extra virgin olive oil
1 tablespoon sherry vinegar
salt and pepper
1 tablespoon soft brown sugar
pinch powdered ginger

accompaniment
2 large chipping potatoes
3 baby artichokes
flour
olive oil, for frying
4 thick slices rustic bread
3 tablespoons herb oil
3 tablespoons black olive oil
4 slices boudin sausage
4 slices Iberian ham, dried in the oven
1 tablespoon reduced sherry
  vinegar

1 PRESERVED PEPPERS
Halve, wash, and deseed the peppers and place in a terrine. Add the oil, vinegar, salt, pepper, sugar, and ginger. Slow bake in the oven at 140°F (60°C) for four hours. Cut into julienne strips.

2
Fill four glass pots two-thirds full with the peppers. Put an egg in each pot, making sure the yolk is centered. Cook in a bain-marie in the oven at 300°F (150°F) for 20 minutes.

1 ACCOMPANIMENT
Cut four thick potato sticks. Poach in olive oil at 195°F (90°C). Just before serving, mandolin the artichokes into chips and coat with flour. Deep-fry the artichokes and potato sticks together at 355°F (180°C).

2
Cut the bread into eight sticks. Brush four sticks with herb oil and four with black olive oil, and crisp under the broiler. Pan-fry the slices of sausage.

3
Garnish each pot with a slice of ham. Drizzle with reduced sherry vinegar and serve with the vegetable, bread, and sausage accompaniment.

RECOMMENDED WINE PEÇASO 2002, BODEGAS TELMO RODRIGUEZ

huevo fogon

fatéma hal
quoting ernest pépin
LE MANSOURIA, PARIS

"reading recreates the soul of things; writing builds a nest for the eggs of the memory."

serves 4

almond-stuffed eggs
6 eggs
¾ cup (80 g) ground almonds
1 pinch salt
1 pinch cinnamon
1 pinch ground nutmeg
1 pinch saffron pistils
1 pinch fine sugar
½ teaspoon orange flower water
meat gravy (optional)
3 tablespoons flour and
  ½ cup (100 ml) water,
  to seal the eggs
whole almonds, to garnish

black cumin omelets
6 eggs
1 teaspoon black cumin
½ teaspoon salt
3 tablespoons (45 ml) oil

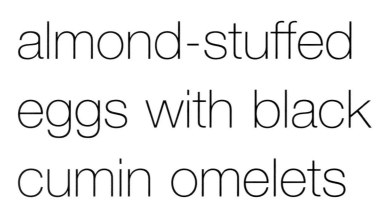

almond-stuffed eggs with black cumin omelets

1 ALMOND-STUFFED EGGS

Wash the eggs. Break two eggs into a mixing bowl and add the almonds, salt, cinnamon, nutmeg, saffron, sugar, and orange-flower water. Mix thoroughly.

2

Prepare a flour-and-water paste for sealing the eggs.

3

One by one, cut a hole at the end of each shell, big enough to fit the nozzle of a piping bag. Drain out the white, leaving the yolk inside. Fill the eggs with the almond stuffing using a piping bag. Plug the shells together again with the flour paste and cook in boiling water or meat gravy for ten minutes. Cool under cold running water.

4

Serve the eggs either in their shells, cut in halves lengthwise, or with the shells removed, cut in the same way. Garnish withe the whole almonds. Serve with the Black Cumin Omelets as an accompaniment for a meat dish or on its own as a starter.

RECOMMENDED WINE KSAR BAHIA RED

1 BLACK CUMIN OMELETS

Beat the eggs in a mixing bowl with the black cumin and salt.

2

Heat the oil in a frying pan and cook the mixture in small amounts to make mini omelets.

RECOMMENDED WINE RIAD JAMIL

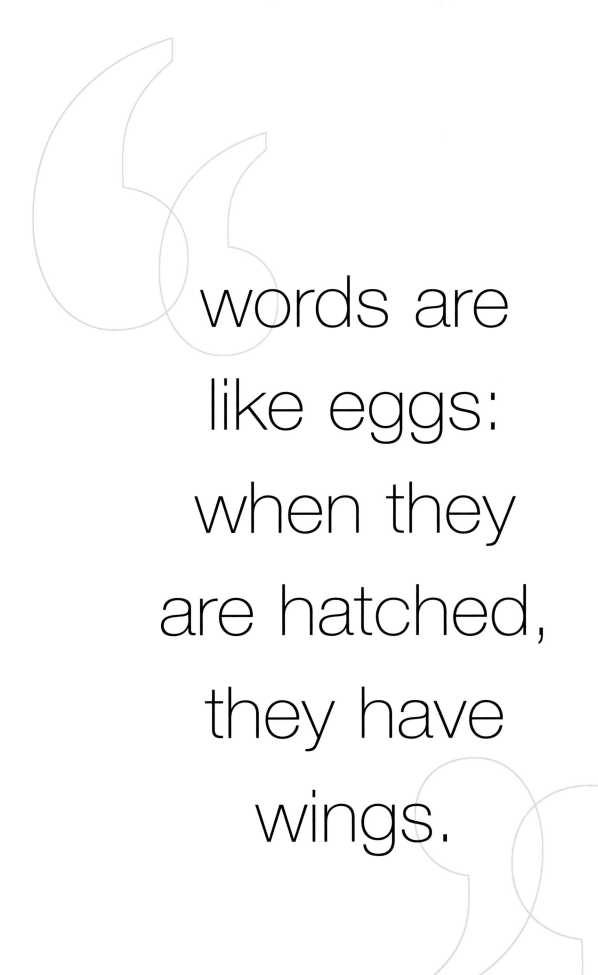

words are
like eggs:
when they
are hatched,
they have
wings.

taïra kurihara
quoting a Malagasy proverb

TAÏRA, PARIS

split scramble
with salmon
and creamed beet

serves 4

salmon
⅓ cup (100 g) salt
¼ cup (50 g) sugar
8 ounces (250 g) raw salmon

creamed beet
1 cooked beet, weighing
   3 ½ ounces (100 g)
2 cups (200 ml) rice milk
juice of half a lemon

scramble
8 eggs
2 cups (200 ml) heavy
   whipping cream
salt and pepper
8 shiso leaves
⅓ cup (100 g) butter

1 SALMON

Combine the salt and sugar, and cover the salmon with this mixture. Leave to penetrate. After 15 to 20 minutes, wipe off with a clean tea towel. Cut the salmon into small cubes
.

2 CREAMED BEET

Cut the cooked beet into small pieces. Liquidize with rice milk. Season with salt and a few drops of lemon juice. Refrigerate.

3 SCRAMBLE

Separate the eggs. Combine half the cream with the yolks in one bowl, and the other half with the whites in another. Season well with salt and pepper. Boil water in a bain-marie. Butter the inner pan. Pour in the yolk mixture, stirring with a spatula, and watch it carefully: it should finish as a loose cream. Repeat the process in another bain-marie with the whites.

4

Spoon the scrambled whites into the bottom of a glass. Add the salmon pieces and a finely chopped shiso leaf. Spoon the scrambled yolks on top, and finish with the creamed beet. Decorate with a shiso leaf.

RECOMMENDED WINE WHITE CÔTE DE BEAUNE,
SAINT-AUBIN 1ER CRU, LE CHARMOIS, OLIVIER LEFLAIVE

" you can only eat a

but you can eat its egg

william ledeuil
quoting a Tajik proverb

ZE KITCHEN GALLERIE, PARIS

chicken once,

a hundred times.

deep-fried breaded
bouillon and udon

serves 4

4 poached eggs

Parmesan bouillon
1 ⅔ cup (300 g) Parmesan
1 ⅓ cups (300 ml) chicken
  bouillon
1 ⅓ cups (300 ml) milk
⅓ cup (70 g) butter
celery salt
cubeb pepper

garnish
10 ounces (300 g) Udon noodles
10 ounces (300 g) chanterelle
  mushrooms
1 ½ tablespoons olive oil
1 red onion
2 stems Thai basil
⅓ cup (75 ml) creamed artichoke
salt and pepper

Japanese crumb
2 egg yolks
⅓ tube karashi (yellow
  Japanese mustard)
½ cup (60 g) flour

crostini
4 slices poppy-seed bread
1 ½ tablespoons olive oil
⅔ cup (150 ml) creamed
  artichoke
3 lengths Chinese spring onion
3 ounces (100 g) chopped
  chanterelle mushrooms

finishing
12 very fine slices chorizo

egg with a parmesan noodles

1 PARMESAN BOUILLON

Grate the Parmesan in a food processor. Add the milk to the chicken bouillon and bring to the boil. Add the Parmesan and whisk over a very low heat. Mix in the butter in small pieces. Season with celery salt and cubeb pepper. Strain and set aside in a warm place.

2 GARNISH

Cook the Udon noodles for two minutes, cool in cold water, and drain. Clean the chanterelles and sauté in olive oil. Add the chopped onion, Thai basil and creamed artichoke. Season and set aside in a warm place.

3 JAPANESE CRUMB

Mix together the egg yolks, karashi, and flour. Coat the poached eggs in this crumb mixture.

3 CROSTINI

Brush the poppy-seed bread with olive oil, and grill. Spread with creamed artichoke and sprinkle with Chinese spring onion and chopped chanterelles.

4 FINISHING

Sauté the noodles with the mushroom mixture and chorizo over a high heat. Add half a ladleful of Parmesan bouillon to coat the noodles. Add seasoning. Deep-fry the poached eggs, but not for too long: the yolk must still be runny. Set a bed of noodles in a soup plate. Emulsify the Parmesan bouillon with a hand blender and pour onto the noodles. Place a deep-fried egg in the middle and serve with crostini.

RECOMMENDED WINE WHITE COTEAUX DU LANGUEDOC, CASCAILLE 2004, DOMAINE CLAVEL

"eggs are at the origin of all the world's cooking. they can do anything!"

jean-françois piège
RESTAURANT LES AMBASSADEURS, HÔTEL DE CRILLON, PARIS

serves 4

chive butter
1 bunch chives
4 tablespoons (40 g) lightly
 salted butter
freshly ground pepper

shell-free eggs
4 eggs
1 pound (500 g) sandwich bread
4 cups groundnut oil, for deep-flying

crayfish
4 crayfish
olive oil
1 clove garlic
¼ bunch parsley
2 tablespoons cognac
1 ½ tablespoons butter
salt and freshly ground pepper

chanterelles, almonds
7 ounces (200 g) small chanterelle
mushrooms (reserve a few
 for finishing)
olive oil
1 ½ tablespoons butter

finishing
12 fresh almonds
salt and freshly ground pepper

shell-free egg with crayfish, chanterelles, almonds

1 CHIVE BUTTER

Chop the chives very finely. Soften the butter. Mix in the chives and add a little freshly ground pepper.

2 MAKING THE "SHELL-FREE" EGGS

Break the eggs cleanly without crushing the shells, and separate them, being careful not to break the yolks. Set aside the whites.

Dry the insides of the eight shell halves and coat them thickly with chive butter. Leave to harden in the freezer.

Peel the eggshell molds off four of the butter "shells," repairing and returning to the freezer as necessary. Put an egg yolk in each of the remaining butter-lined half shells. Place a butter-only shell on top and seal the two halves with butter. Leave to harden again in the freezer. Peel off the remaining shell and smooth over the join. Beat the egg whites and make breadcrumbs with the fresh sandwich bread. Coat the butter eggs with two layers of egg white and breadcrumbs. Leave to rest in the refrigerator for about an hour.

3 CRAYFISH

Separate the crayfish tails from the heads. Roast the tails in a cast-iron casserole with a drizzle of olive oil for three minutes. Remove from heat, add crushed garlic and parsley, and deglaze with cognac. Cover with a damp tea towel and leave for 15 minutes to infuse. Shell the tails. Sear the tails in butter, season with salt and freshly ground pepper.

4 CHANTERELLES AND ALMONDS

Clean the chanterelles, wash in plenty of water, and drain. Sear once in olive oil to release the juices, then drain. Sear again in browned butter, and season with salt and freshly ground black pepper.

5 FINISHING

Deep-fry the eggs in groundnut oil at 390°F (200°C), giving a pretty light-brown color. Drain on kitchen paper and leave under a very low grill to harden the crust. Season with salt and freshly ground pepper. Balance a crayfish, a fresh almond, and a slice of chanterelle on top of the breaded egg, and serve immediately.

RECOMMENDED WINE PULIGNY-MONTRACHET, 1ER CRU "LES COMBETTES" 2000, DOMAINE JACQUES PRIEUR

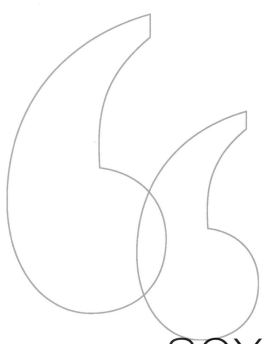

sex without sin

is like an egg

without salt.

alain passard
quoting carlos fuentes
L'ARPÈGE, PARIS

serves 4

8 eggs
4 tablespoons (40 g) salted butter
unrefined sea salt
4 slices bread (for soldiers)

eggs sunny-side inside

1
Melt a tablespoonful of butter over a low heat in each of the serving dishes. When the butter froths, delicately break an egg on the edge of the dish.

2
Let the white run into the dish, but keep the yolk in the shell.

3
Place the half-shell containing the yolk onto the white. Cook over a low heat for five to seven minutes.

4
Sprinkle a few salt crystals on the yolk.

Before serving, the yolk can be tipped onto the white, or left in its shell. Serve with generously buttered soldiers.

RECOMMENDED WINE WHITE SAUMUR, CHÂTEAU YVONNE 2002

"put all your eggs in one

basket and…
watch that basket!

roland durand
quoting mark twain

LE PASSIFLORE, PARIS

1 EGGS "HUNDRED-YEAR" STYLE

The day before serving, boil two quarts of water with the turmeric, the cinnamon, coriander seeds, and saffron. Cook the eggs for five minutes in this liquid, remove and cool quickly in iced water.

2

Leave the cooking liquid from the eggs to cool in a bowl. Break the shell of the egg by tapping it lightly on a hard surface as if you were about to peel it, but leave it covered in its cracked shell. Leave the eggs to sit in the cooled cooking liquid covered in the refrigerator overnight.

1 TAJINE

Carefully peel the eggs and set aside.

2

Cut the potato into tiny dice.

3

Blanch the ducks' tongues, drain, and brown in the olive oil. Add the chopped onion and cook until it turns a pale golden color. Add the garlic, ginger, powdered cumin, and a pinch of saffron, then finish with the lemon juice and chicken stock. Cook gently for forty minutes and check for seasoning.

4

Boil two quarts of water with the salt. Add in the pak-choi, pea flowers, and fava beans. After 30 seconds, drain and refresh the vegetables quickly in iced water, but do not leave them sitting in the water.

5

Reheat the eggs gently in a steamer for five minutes. Reheat the vegetables with the ducks' tongues.

6

Arrange the ducks' tongues and the vegetables in individual tajine dishes. Place the eggs in the centre of each dish and decorate with the jalapeno peppers and diced potato.

RECOMMENDED WINE CONDIEU 2002, PIERRE GAILLARD

serves 4

eggs "hundred-year" style
4 large eggs
1 tablespoon fresh turmeric, peeled and chopped
1 small stick cinnamon
1 tablespoon coriander seeds
1 pinch powdered saffron

tajine of ducks' tongues
1 small blue potato (also known as purple or black potatoes), boiled and left to cool
32 ducks' tongues
3 ½ tablespoons (50 ml) olive oil
1 small onion, chopped
1 garlic clove, chopped fine
1 tablespoon fresh ginger, finely chopped
1 pinch powdered cumin pinch saffron
juice of 1 lemon
2 cups (500 ml) chicken stock
1 large tablespoon salt
16 miniature pak-choi
12 pea flowers
1 tablespoon small fava beans
12 small medium-hot jalapeno peppers finely chopped

tajine of ducks' tongues
with eggs "hundred-year" style

a home without a grandmother is like an egg without salt.

fried eggs with
and lotus flowers

sorrel cream

serves 4

soft-boiled eggs
3 eggs

sorrel cream
fresh sorrel
¼ cup (50 ml) water
scant cup (200 ml) grape seed oil
3 tablespoons (45 ml) olive oil

fried eggs
4 fresh eggs
1 ½ tablespoons butter

yellow leaves
sprigs of chervil
lotus flowers
pansies

1 SOFT-BOILED EGGS
Boil the eggs for three minutes, starting in cold water. Drain and refresh in iced water before peeling carefully. Set aside.

2 SORREL CREAM
Blend the sorrel with the water, add the soft-boiled eggs and then add the grape seed oil in a trickle as if making a mayonnaise. Finish the sauce with the olive oil, strain through a fine sieve, and store in the refrigerator.

3 LEAVES
Pick over the herbs and flowers and keep them on a damp paper towel.

4 FRIED EGGS
Melt the butter in a cast-iron egg dish on the stove. Break the eggs and slip them gently into the dish. Cook for six to seven minutes, making sure that the yolk is in the center of the egg. Leave to rest for a moment before shaping with an oval cookie-cutter.

5 FINISHING
Spoon the sauce delicately onto the plate, slide the egg carefully on the sauce, and decorate with the herbs and freshly picked flowers.

RECOMMENDED WINE MACON-BUISSIÈRES, DOMAINE DE LA SARAZINIÈRE, VIEILLES VIGNES 2004

soft snow with red

Recipe by Pascal Goutaudier, head pastry

serves 4

12 empty eggshells
(see method opposite)

soft snow
generous half cup (125 g)
of egg whites
11 tablespoons (90 g)
confectioners' sugar

pistachio ice-cream
2 cups (450 ml) milk
3 ½ tablespoons (50 ml) cup
heavy cream
2 ¼ tablespoons (50 ml) inverted
sugar syrup*
½ cup (100 g) granulated sugar
scant ½ cup (60 g)
powdered glucose
¼ cup (50 g) green pistachio paste

red fruits
raspberries
wild strawberries

to finish
pansies
bee balm
verbena
rose petals
calendula
pistachios
candied lemon peel
raspberry coulis

* see glossary, page 190

fruits and flowers

cook at Restaurant Jean Brouilly

1 EMPTY EGGSHELLS

Empty the eggs using a special egg cutter and scoop out the inside. Keep the eggs for another recipe and delicately clean the shell, removing all traces of the white membrane that lines the shell. Wash the shells and sterilize them in a steamer for ten minutes at 250° F (115° C). Set aside.

2 SOFT SNOW

Whisk the egg whites into soft peaks, adding the sugar progressively as for a meringue, then stir the whites gently a few times and transfer to a piping bag. Pipe the meringue into the eggshells and steam for five minutes at 175° F (80°C). Gently break and remove the eggshells, making sure not to damage the cooked meringue inside. Tidy the base of each egg so that it sits flat, using a thin-bladed knife, and keep in the refrigerator

3 PISTACHIO ICE-CREAM

Warm the milk with the cream and the inverted sugar syrup. Mix the sugar and glucose with a whisk and pour onto the warmed milk before bringing to the boil. Gently mix the pistachio paste into the milk, strain through a fine sieve, and leave to cool to 40 °F (4° C) before freezing in an ice-cream machine.

4 PREPARING THE FRUITS

Cut the strawberries and the larger raspberries in half.

5 PREPARING THE FLOWERS

Pick over the herbs and flowers and keep them on a damp paper towel.

6 FINISHING

Using a roof slate as a dish, create a little nest of red fruits and position three "soft snow" meringues on each. Decorate with the flower petals. On the side, place five half raspberries garnished with pistachio and candied lemon peel. Dribble the raspberry coulis in drops around the dish and finish with a scoop of pistachio ice-cream.

RECOMMENDED WINE COTEAUX DE L'AUBANCE, CUVÉE HARMONIE 2002, MAURICE FOREST

you can

enjoy

an egg

a hundred

times more

than a hen.

flora mikula

LES SAVEURS DE FLORA, PARIS, FRANCE

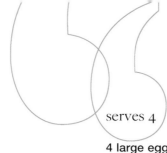

serves 4

4 large eggs
4 cups (1 l) chicken stock
6 tablespoons (70 g) unsweetened peanut butter
oil and butter for cooking the mushrooms
scant ½ pound (200 g) shitake mushrooms, sliced
1 shallot
1 clove garlic
generous ½ cup (100 g) grilled peanuts, roughly chopped
2 leaves gelatin
7 tablespoons (100 ml) wine vinegar
½ –1 (120–250ml) cup pouring cream
½ teaspoon wasabi*
4 slices toasted bread
3 tablespoons (30 g) smooth peanut butter

chaud-froid of eggs with shitake mushrooms in peanut aspic and peanut butter toast

1

Boil the chicken stock with the unsweetened peanut butter and strain through a fine sieve. Heat the oil and butter in a hot skillet and fry the mushrooms, shallots and garlic.

2

Add the chopped peanuts and ¾ of the chicken stock mixture. Leave to simmer for a good five minutes before adding the gelatin leaves. Soak the gelatin leaves then add the stock.

3

Divide half the mushroom mixture among four Martini glasses.

4

Bring a pan of water with a little vinegar to the boil and poach the eggs one by one for three minutes each. Drain on paper towels. Place one in each glass and cover with the remaining mushroom mixture.

5

In a separate saucepan, reduce by half the remaining chicken stock, the cream, and the wasabi. Blend thoroughly and spoon the foam on top of each glass.

6

Serve with the toast smeared with peanut butter.

RECOMMENDED WINE VAL BRUYÈRE, BLANC DE CASSIS, LE CLOS VAL BRUYÈRE, SOPHIE CERCIELLO, CASSIS

* see glossary, page 190

"even if you spend your life working as a cook you will never exhaust all the possibilities in an egg."

pascal barbot

L'ASTRANCE, PARIS

serves 4

4 eggs
2 cups (500 ml) mineral water
2 bay leaves
2 ½ tablespoons turmeric
fleur de sel* (coarse salt)
olive oil

garnish

1 ½ tablespoons diced
   red bell pepper
¼ pound young cauliflower
   florets
6 tablespoons (20 g) chopped
   green onion

decoration

fleur de sel
freshly ground black pepper
juice of one lemon
1 ½ tablespoons capers
olive oil
borage
fresh savory
tarragon
purple shiso leaves

slightly "cracked" eggs

1 EGGS
Cook the eggs in boiling water for six minutes, drain, and refresh in iced water. Using a spoon, tap the eggs to "crack" the shells.

2
Bring the mineral water to the boil, add the bay leaf and turmeric, and leave to cool. Add the eggs and leave overnight in the refrigerator. Peel the eggs, season with the salt and olive oil, and serve with the garnish below.

3 GARNISH
Pick over and wash the ingredients for the garnish, leaving them to soak for ten minutes in iced water. Dress like any other salad, using the salt, pepper, lemon juice, capers, and olive oil. Finish by adding the borage, savory, tarragon, and shiso.

RECOMMENDED WINE A *VIN JAUNE* FROM ARBOIS IN THE JURA; DOMAINE DE STÉPHANE ET BÉNÉDICTE TISSOT

* see glossary, page 190

dan barber
quoting max favalelli

BLUE HILL, STONE BARNS, USA

"I have

never

laid

an egg in

my life…

but

I still think

I'm better

qualified

to judge

an omelet

than a hen is.

serves 4

4 eggs
4 pieces edible gold leaf

lentils
¾ cup (160 g) beluga lentils
2 teaspoons olive oil
1 onion, cut into tiny dice
  the size of the lentils
bouquet garni composed of:
  ½ medium carrot, peeled and
  cut in half lengthways
  ½ celery stick, peeled and
  cut in half lengthways
  1 sprig of thyme
  ½ bay leaf
2 teaspoons red wine vinegar
salt and pepper

gilded
eggs

1 LENTILS
Wash the lentils thoroughly.

2
Sweat the onion gently in the olive oil over a gentle heat.

3
In a medium-sized saucepan, sweat the lentils over moderate heat for two or three minutes, stirring constantly to ensure they do not stick. Add the cooked onion, two glasses of water, and the bouquet garni, season with salt, and stir until it comes to the boil.

4
Leave the lentils to cook for fifteen to twenty minutes, then drain.

5
Add the red wine vinegar and season to taste.

1 EGGS
Cook the eggs in salted boiling water for four to five minutes.

2
Refresh in iced water.

3
With the aid of a spoon, crack and remove the shell.

Arrange a small pile of lentils in each dish, sit the egg on top and crown with a piece of gold leaf. Serve immediately.

RECOMMENDED WINE GRAVES BLANC

"love is a freshly laid egg,

pierre hermé
quoting fr. oliban

PARIS (FRANCE), TOKYO (JAPAN)

marriage a hard-boiled egg,
and divorce a scrambled egg.

isaphan tart

For 12 individual tarts

sweet pastry
1 ⅓ cups (300 g) butter
¾ cup (60 g) ground almonds
1 ½ cups (190 g) icing sugar
¼ teaspoon powdered vanilla
6 egg yolks
pinch of coarse salt
1 pound (500 g) plain white flour

egg cream and rose-flavored cream cheese
5 cups (1.2 l) heavy cream
scant ½ pound (220 g)
    Philadelphia cream cheese
6 tablespoons (100 g) egg yolks
1 ¼ tablespoons superfine sugar
1 ¼ teaspoons natural rose
    flavoring (Sévarome)
¼ cup rose syrup
1 leaf finest quality gelatin

litchi aspic
1 ¾ tablespoons
    superfine sugar
½–¾ teaspoon gellan
    (gelling agent)
½ pound (500 g) puréed litchis
¼ teaspoon natural rose flavoring
    (Sévarome)
scant 1 ½ tablespoons
    lemon juice

isaphan macaroon sponge
¼ pound (100 g) whole almonds,
    ground to a powder
2 ½ cup (200 g) confectioners'
    sugar
2 ½ tablespoons (35 g)
    fresh egg whites
¾ teaspoon carmine red
    food coloring
generous cup (250 ml) water
3 tablespoons (40 g) "old" egg
    whites (left at room temperature
    for twenty-four hours)

preparation and finishing
cooked sweet pastry bases
rose-flavored cream cheese
20 fresh raspberries
cubes of litchi aspic
raspberry jelly
rose petals
rose-flavored glucose syrup

with eggs

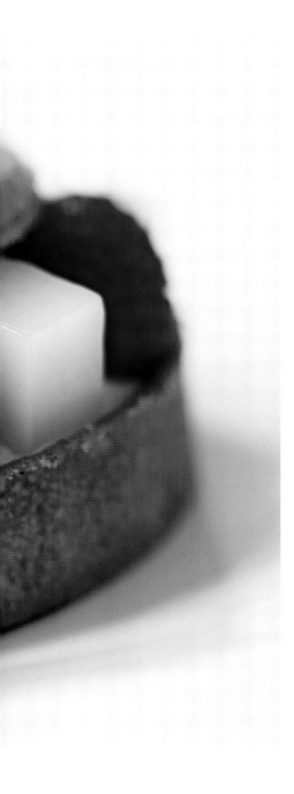

1 SWEET PASTRY
Work the butter to soften it, then add the ingredients one by one in the order listed opposite. Wrap in food wrap and refrigerate for at least two hours. Roll the pastry to ⅛ inch (2 mm) and cut into five-inch (13-cm) disks. Store on a baking sheet in the refrigerator for 30 minutes. Grease the insides of twelve pastry rings, five inches (13 cm) wide by ¾ inch (2 cm) deep and line them with the pastry, removing any excess. Arrange on silicone paper and store in the refrigerator. Line the tarts with silicone paper, fill with baking beans, and bake at 335° F (170 °C) for twenty to 20 to 25 minutes. Remove the baking beans when cooked.

2 EGG CREAM AND ROSE-FLAVORED CREAM CHEESE
Bring the cream to the boil with the cream cheese. Add the egg yolks and sugar, the natural rose flavoring, and the rose syrup and cook as for a custard. Add the gelatin. Cool quickly and store in the refrigerator.

3 LITCHI ASPIC
Mix the gellan and sugar and incorporate into the litchi purée at 113°F (45°C). Raise the temperature to 185°F (85°C), stirring regularly. Add the rose flavor and blend to produce a homogenous mass. Line the base of a rectangular dish 8 x 6 inches (30 x 15 cm) with silicone paper and pour the litchi mixture in directly. Leave to cool in the refrigerator. Unmold by turning it onto a sheet of silicone paper. Using a sharp knife cut ¾-inch (2-cm) cubes from the aspic and store in the refrigerator.

4 ISAPHAN MACAROON SPONGE
Mix the ground almonds and confectioners' sugar with the "fresh" egg whites and the coloring. Cook the confectioners' sugar and water to 243°F (117°C). When the sugar reaches 226°F (108°C) start beating the "old" egg whites. When the whites are stiff, but not yet too firm, pour in the sugar in a thin stream, stirring constantly and leave to cool to 120°F (50°C), stirring all the time. Incorporate this (it is called Italian meringue) into the first mixture; let the mixture "fall" a little before forming 2 ½-inch (6-cm) disks on a Silipat baking sheet using a stencil made from stiff cardboard. Smooth the surface with a palette knife and cook in a convector oven at 320°F (160°C), for ten minutes with the door of the oven slightly open.

5 ASSEMBLY AND PRESENTATION
Using a piping bag fitted with a N°12 nozzle, fill the pastry cases with rose-flavored cream cheese so that it extends well above the edge of the case. Spread a thin layer of raspberry jelly over the surface and alternate raspberries and cubes of litchi aspic until you reach the centre of the tart. Place a rose-flavored macaroon in the center of each and decorate with a red rose petal and a droplet of rose-flavored glucose syrup.

if eggs were square, the hen's life would be hell.

alfred prasad

TAMARIND, LONDON, ENGLAND

serves 4

4 eggs
generous ¾ cup (200 ml) milk
2 medium sized onions
2 mild green chili peppers
6 tomatoes
piece of fresh ginger root,
 about 1 inch (2.5 cm) long
1 bunch coriander
2 ½ tablespoons vegetable oil
2 tablespoons turmeric
2 tablespoons ground
 chili powder
salt
toast or chapatis, for serving

1

Beat the eggs with the milk.

2

Peel the onions and slice them thinly along with the
green chili peppers. Wash and slice four tomatoes
into rounds. Set aside.

3

Peel the ginger and slice into thin matchsticks.

4

Carefully wash and chop the coriander.

5

Heat the oil in a nonstick skillet; sweat the onions
and chili peppers gently, until the onions become
transparent.

6

Add the ginger, turmeric, and chili powder and
cook for a further five minutes.

7

Next add the tomatoes slices, and cook until they
have reduced to a thick purée. Add a little water if
necessary.

8

Add the egg and milk mixture, season with salt, stir,
and cook until the eggs have set.

9

Finally, add the chopped coriander. Serve
accompanied with the remaining fresh tomatoes,
and toast or chapatis.

RECOMMENDED ACCOMPANIMENT
BLACK ASSAM TEA, SECOND FLUSH

masala egg bhurjee

(an indian breakfast)

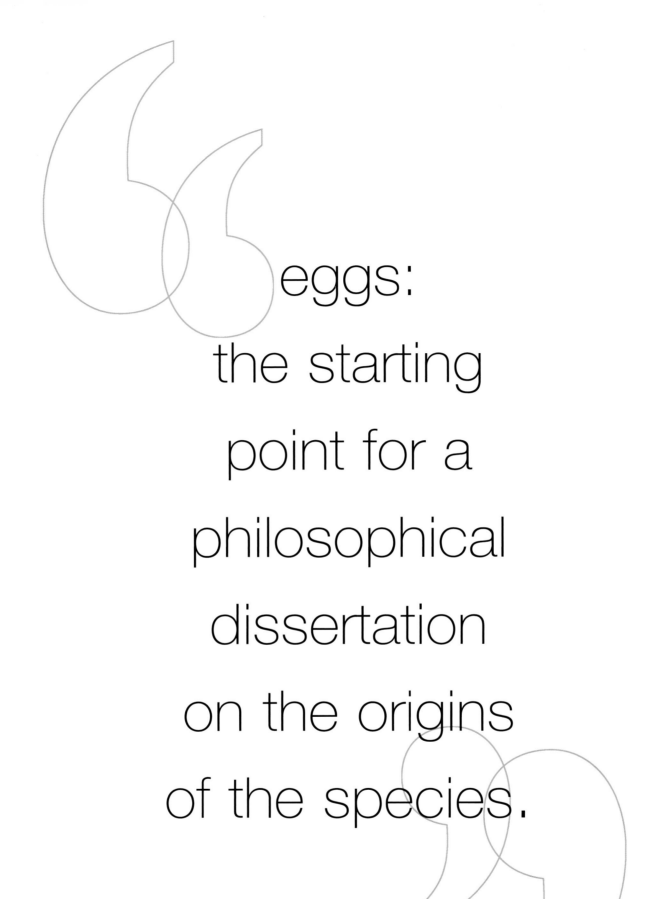

"eggs:
the starting
point for a
philosophical
dissertation
on the origins
of the species."

yves camdeborde
quoting gustave flaubert

LE COMPTOIR, HÔTEL SAINT-GERMAIN, PARIS

serves 4

4 large eggs
¾ pound (400 g) long macaroni
generous ½ pound (300 g)
  fresh black truffles
scant ½ cup (100 g) butter
7 tablespoons (100 ml)
  pouring cream
salt and pepper

1

Cook the macaroni and stuff them with matchsticks of fresh truffle. Refrigerate. Make a hole in the top of the eggs and drain out the inside, taking every precaution not to damage the shells. Reserve the insides and wash the shells in warm water.

2

Slice the macaroni into thin slices, ⅛ inch (2 mm) thick. Line the inside of the eggshells with the slices and refrigerate.

3

Scramble the eggs. Melt a little butter in a saucepan, and add the eggs, cream, and remaining butter as well as the remaining chopped truffles. Season well with salt and pepper. Put the saucepan into a boiling double-boiler. Stir with a spatula. Towards the end, make sure the eggs remain soft and creamy.

4

Stuff the four eggs with the scrambled eggs and refrigerate for one hour. To serve, delicately remove the shell.

RECOMMENDED WINE DOMAINE DE LA ROMANÉE CONTI, 1964

hen's egg "guy legay"

éric frechon
quoting francis blanche

LE BRISTOL, PARIS

"he that
will steal
an egg
will steal
an ox."

boiled free-range hen's egg with garden peas, chorizo, sausage, roast sobrasada sausage, and nasturtium flower foam

1 PREPARATION
Remove the top of the egg shells and carefully drain out the insides. Wash and dry the egg shells.

2 SCRAMBLED EGGS
Cook the scrambled eggs until quite stiff. Blend with the butter and cream and season, then pour into a siphon* and keep warm in a double boiler.

3 GARNISH
Sweat the green onions in butter, moisten slightly with pale stock and cook until it has boiled off, then add the garden peas and the finely diced chorizo.

4 NASTURTIUM FOAM
Cook all the vegetables with the pale stock and water. Cook gently for one hour. Strain off the stock and blend with the nasturtiums, saffron, and cream. Gently sweat the rabbit carcass without letting it color, and add the flavored stock. Strain this mixture and keep in a siphon.

5 SOBRASSADA TOASTS
Use the siphon to fill the eggshell with a layer of the vegetable garnish followed by a layer of egg, and top with a crown of nasturtium foam. Spread the sobrassada on slices of the country-style baguette and brown in the oven for two minutes before serving. Cut each slice in half before arranging on the plate.

RECOMMENDED WINE FINO DEL LAGAR, BODEGAS, TORO ALBALA

serves 4

scrambled eggs
12 eggs
¾–1 cup (200 g) butter
¾–1 cup (200 ml) pouring cream
salt and pepper

garnish
1 ½ ounces (40 g) chopped
  green onions
3 tablespoons (120 ml) butter
½ cup pale stock*
2 ounces (60 g) garden peas
1 ½ ounces (35 g) chorizo
  sausage, finely diced

nasturtium flower foam
½ pound (250 g) carrots
scant ½ pound (200 g) onions
5 ounces (150 g) celery
1 ⅓ cups (300 ml) pale stock
1 ⅓ cups (300 ml) water
20 nasturtium flowers
1 teaspoon (350 g) saffron
¾–1 (200 ml) cup pouring cream
¾ pound (350 g) rabbit bones

sobrassada toasts
2 ounces (60 g) sobrassada
3 ounces (80 g) country-style
  baguette

* see glossary, page 190

"sheer perfection, the epitome of form, minimalist and yet elegant, fragile yet strong;

besides being the shape of the philosopher's stone, eggs are also the basis of everything culinary.

patrice hardy

LA TRUFFE NOIR, NEUILLY-SUR-SEINE, FRANCE

12 eggs
½ cup (120 g) black truffles
⅓ cup (80 g) butter
bread for toasted "soldiers"
salt and freshly ground
  black pepper
¾–1 cup (200 ml) concentrated
  dark chicken gravy made
  from a roast chicken
fleur de sel* (coarse salt)
splash of olive oil flavored
  with garlic

scrambled eggs with truffles

1 THE DAY BEFORE

Clean and open the eggs carefully on top, pouring the contents of each egg into a plastic bowl with ⅔ of the truffles, chopped finely, and half the butter in pieces. Mix well and close the bowl with a tight-fitting lid.

2 ON THE DAY

Chop the rest of the truffles, then cut the bread into "soldiers" and fry them. Smear half of them with the softened butter, then roll them in the chopped truffle. Heat the chicken gravy, add a knob of butter and any remaining chopped truffle.

3 COOKING

Use a heavy sauté pan, preferably in copper, cover the inside in butter and add the egg mixture from the night before. Season with the coarse salt and cook in a double boiler, stirring constantly, until you reach a creamy consistency. Remove from the heat, add the rest of the butter and stir energetically. Check the seasoning and add a splash of garlic-flavored olive oil.

4 FINISHING AND SERVING

Arrange the eggshells on the dish in the form of an artist's palette. Fill with the truffled scrambled eggs and pour a spoon of the concentrated, truffle-flavored chicken gravy into each egg before placing the "soldiers" attractively on the plate.

RECOMMENDED WINE POMEROL, CHÂTEAU LA CONSEILLANTE, 1998

* see glossary, page 190

hirohisa koyama
quoting arnold h. glasgow

LE AOYAGI, TOKYO, JAPAN

" the key to everything is
chicken by hatching the

patience. you get the
egg, not by smashing it.

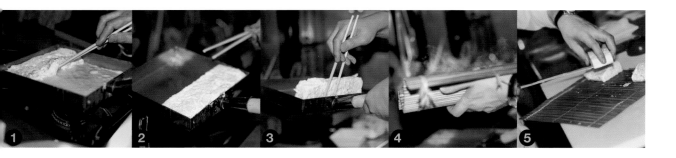

tamago yaki no tsukuri

kata (rolled omelet with tsukuda-ni)

Eat this omelet warm, as the bouillion inside has a tendency to seep out as it cools.
Serve the omelet with the tsukuda-ni as an accomaniment.

serves 4

6 eggs
½ cup (120 ml) dashi (see below)
dash of light soy sauce
pinch of salt
3 tablespoons (50 ml) sunflower oil
wasabi*, for serving

koyama-style dashi
1 teaspoon kombu seaweed
   (4 x 2 inch/10 x 5 cm leaves)
½ ounce (15 g) katsuobushi
   (parings of dried bonito)
4 cups (1 l) water

tsukuda-ni
leftover kombu and bonito parings
2 tablespoons light soy sauce
scant ½ cup (100 ml) water
dash of sake

* see glossary, page 190

1 ROLLED OMELET

In a bowl, mix the cooled dashi stock (see method below) with the light soy sauce and salt until completely dissolved.

2

Break the eggs into a bowl, whisk with the chopsticks but without letting them foam, and add the dashi stock, soy sauce, and salt preparation. Strain through a fine sieve.

3

Generously oil a rectangular Japanese skillet, or if you do not have one, an ordinary round skillet, and heat over moderate heat. Pour one-third of the preparation in the pan and spread it evenly. When it is half-cooked, using chopsticks, fold in it three towards you **(1)**.

4

Using a paper towel soaked in oil, grease the exposed part of the skillet then slide the omelet onto this part of the pan **(2)**.

5

Oil the exposed part of the pan (closest to you) as before and pour half the remaining mixture into the pan, letting it slip slightly under the previously cooked omelet. When it is half set, repeat the same operation as above, then do the same with the remaining mixture **(3)**.

6

Place the omelet on a bamboo (makisu) mat and form it into a rectangle (or roll, if you used a round skillet). Leave to rest for three or four minutes **(4)**.

7

Cut the omelet into 1 ¼-inch (3-cm) slices and arrange on a dish with wasabi and the tsukuda-ni **(5)**.

1 KOYAMA-STYLE DASHI (KOMBU SEAWEED AND KATSUOBUSHI STOCK)

Wipe the surface of the kombu seaweed with a damp cloth to remove the dust, but keep the white powder that is stuck to it, which is where the flavor lies.

2

Heat the water, and add the kombu seaweed when it begins to simmer.

3

When it starts to simmer again, add the katsuobushi. Leave to simmer gently for three minutes.

4

Remove from the heat and leave the dried tuna to fall to the bottom before straining through a very fine sieve.

1 TSUKUDA-NI (BONITO PARINGS AND KOMBU, BARELY SOFT-COOKED)

The soft-cooked seaweed and bonito is made using the leftovers from the dashi. Cut the kombu seaweed into squares.

2

In a small saucepan, mix the chopped seaweed, the bonito parings, the soy sauce, water, and sake.

3

Squash the bonito parings.

4

Leave to simmer on moderate heat until all the liquid has evaporated.

RECOMMENDED WINE SAKE "KINPÛ"

jean-luc poujauran

PAIN POUJAURAN DIFFUSION, PARIS, FRANCE

"half an egg

is better than

an empty

eggcup."

serves 4

2 whole eggs plus 1 yolk
2 cups (500 ml) milk
1 ¾ cups (225 g) superfine sugar
3 ½ tablespoons (50 g) butter
1 pod Tahiti vanilla
4 tablespoons (60 ml) Armagnac
½ cup (100 g) sifted plain flour

*These little cakes are made in a traditonal mold.
If cannelé molds are unavailble use other small
cake molds.*

1 THE DAY BEFORE

Boil the milk with half the sugar, whisking from the
base of the saucepan. Remove from the heat, and
add the butter and the vanilla pod, split lengthways
using the tip of a sharp knife.

2

Break the eggs into a mixing bowl and add the egg
yolk. Whisk with the remainder of the sugar until the
mixture whitens. Add the flour and mix through.
Pour in the boiled milk mixture with the remaining
sugar, strain through a fine sieve and refrigerate
for twelve hours. Scrape any remaining seeds
from the vanilla pod using a little knife and add
them to the mixture.

1 ON THE DAY

Cool the molds in the refrigerator. Butter the insides
and fill each with three-quarters of the mixture.

2

Cook for 50 to 55 minutes at 350° F (180° C).

3

Unmold when still hot and leave to cool on a wire rack.

cannelés

"better an egg in peacetime than an ox in war."

sam mason

WD50, NEW YORK

crème brûlée in

serves 4

basic crème brûlée
2 pints (950 ml) cream
1 cup (230 g) sugar
⅓ ounce (10 g) vanilla pod
11 fluid ounces (320 ml) egg yolk

tubes and pearls of crème brûlée
1 teaspoon agar-agar*
generous ½ teaspoon carob flour
5 fluid ounces (150 ml) water
11 fluid ounces (325 ml) of basic crème brûlée preparation
vegetable oil

cocoa caramel
5 fluid ounces (150 ml) water
1 cup (200 g) superfine sugar
½ cup (120 g) glucose
2 tablespoons cocoa

* see glossary, page 190

1 CRÈME-BRÛLÉE TUBES
Dissolve ½ teaspoon agar and ½ teaspoon carob flour in the water and cook gently for five minutes.

2
Heat the basic crème-brulée preparation and mix the agar-agar carob flour preparation into it.

3
Fill flexible pastry tubes with the mixture while it is still hot and leave to set in the refrigerator.

1 CRÈME BRÛLÉE "PEARLS"
Using another 11 fluid ounces (325 g) of the basic preparation, repeat steps one and two above.

2
While it is still hot, fill squeegee bottles with this mixture.

3
Drop "pearls" of this mixture into the vegetable oil, chilled to 50°F (10°C), where they will take shape.

4
After four minutes, use a skimmer to remove the "pearls," and rinse under warm water.

1 COCOA CARAMEL
Bring the water to the boil and mix in the sugar, glucose, and cocoa.

2
Heat over gentle heat for a few minutes, until it caramelizes.

1 FINISHING
Arrange the tubes and pearls of crème brûlée on dishes and flash them quickly under a hot grill until they caramelize.

2
Dribble a little cocoa-flavored caramel on one side of the dish.

RECOMMENDED WINE COTEAUX DE LAYON

two styles: pearls and tubes

"the public thinks that books, like eggs, should be consumed when they are fresh. that is why they always choose to read what is new."

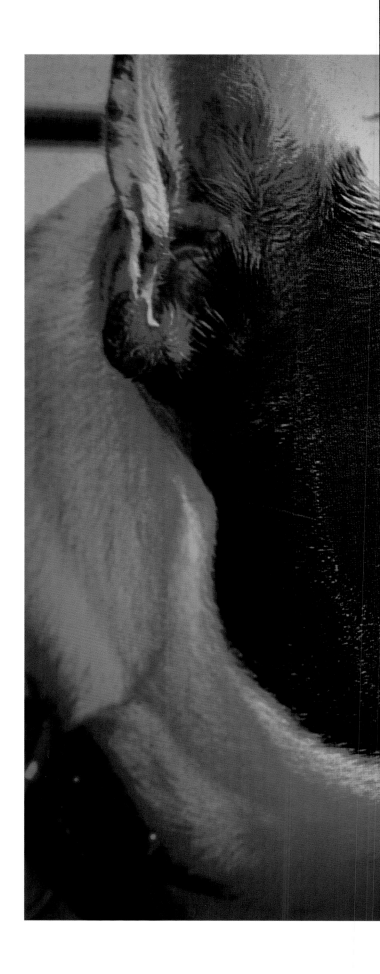

ferran adrià
quoting goethe
EL BULLI, ROSES, SPAIN

*How to caramelize
a quail's egg*

Serves 4

toffee
1 ¾ tablespoons glucose
scant 2 ounces (50 g) fondant
1 ¾ tablespoons Iso-malt*

golden toffee "tiles"
3 ½ tablespoons (50 g) toffee,
   prepared previously
¼ teaspoon edible gold powder

quail's egg yolk
4 quail's eggs
1 ¾ tablespoons sunflower oil
fleur de sel* (coarse salt)
nutmeg
freshly ground black pepper

* see glossary, page 190

golden egg

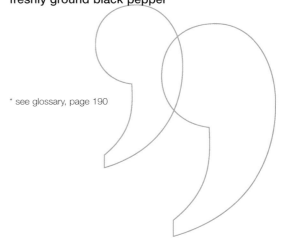

1 TOFFEE
In a small saucepan, heat the glucose and fondant over a gentle heat. Remove from the heat when everything has melted and add the Iso-malt.

2
Cook over moderate heat until the temperature reaches 320°F (160°C). It will rise the last five degrees or so on its own.

3
Remove from the heat and pour on to silicone paper to a depth of ½–¾ inch (1–2 cm). When it reaches the right temperature, cut the caramel into two-inch (5 x 5 cm) squares and set aside.

1 TOFFEE TILES
Place a toffee between two nonstick Silpat baking mats and bake in a 338°F (170°C) oven on a baking tray.

2
Leave for five minutes in the oven until the toffee is malleable then, using a rolling pin, roll into a fine wafer.

3
Place a sheet of silicone paper on the baking tray.

4
Using a brush, paint the toffee square with the gold powder.

5
Put back in the oven and cut into thin waters ¾-inch (2-cm) square.

1 QUAIL'S EGG YOLK
Separate the whites from the yolks, and keep the yolks covered in sunflower oil in a bowl. Put a nonstick Silpat baking mat on a baking tray.

2
Place an egg yolk, making sure it is well covered in sunflower oil, on the Silpat baking mat **(1)** and sit a toffee tile on top with the golden side face upwards **(2)**.

3
Heat under the grill until the toffee melts **(3)** and sticks to the egg yolk

4
Turn the egg yolk over **(4)** on the Silpat, place another tile **(5)** on the opposite side and repeat the procedure. Season with the coarse salt, nutmeg, and black pepper.

To melt the toffee on the egg you can also use a blowtorch. Once caramelized, paint it with the gold powder using a paintbrush.

RECOMMENDED WINE GOSSETT
CHAMPAGNE, GRANDE MILLÉSIME

homogeneity is about as

jean-marie baudic
quoting lawrence durrell

LE YUPALA BISTROT, SAINT-BRIEUC, FRANCE

boring as a statue to an egg.

duck's egg in a zucchini flower shell, with raw vegetable condiment and iced russian tea

1

Coddle the duck eggs in their shell for 1 hour at 320°F (160°C). Carefully wash the zucchini flowers. Extract the egg yolks and put one in each zucchini flower.

2 VEGETABLE CONDIMENT

Chop the carrot and the black and red radish into tiny dice, add the grated broccoli florets, the grilled chopped hazelnuts and the snipped chives, olive oil and, at the last moment, the coarse salt and roughly ground black pepper.

3

Cut the bread into fine slices, spread with olive oil and grill.

4

Slice the zucchinis lengthways and season with a few drops of lemon juice, salt, and pepper.

5

Leave the Russian tea to infuse in water boiled to 160° F (70°C) for two minutes. Cool it quickly and serve very cold.

RECOMMENDED WINE PESSAC-LÉOGNAN 2003, CHÂTEAU COUCHEROY, ANDRÉ LURTON, LÉOGNAN

serves 4

4 duck eggs
4 zucchini flowers
½ poppy seed baguette
3 ½ (45 ml) tablespoons olive oil
½ lemon
salt and pepper
1 teaspoon Russian tea

vegetable condiment
1 carrot
¾ ounce (20 g) black radish
¾ ounce (20 g) red radish
½ head of broccoli, divided
  into florets
2 teaspoons chopped hazelnuts
¼ bunch snipped chives
olive oil
½ teaspoon fleur de sel*
  (coarse salt)
¼ teaspoon peppercorns

* see glossary, page 190

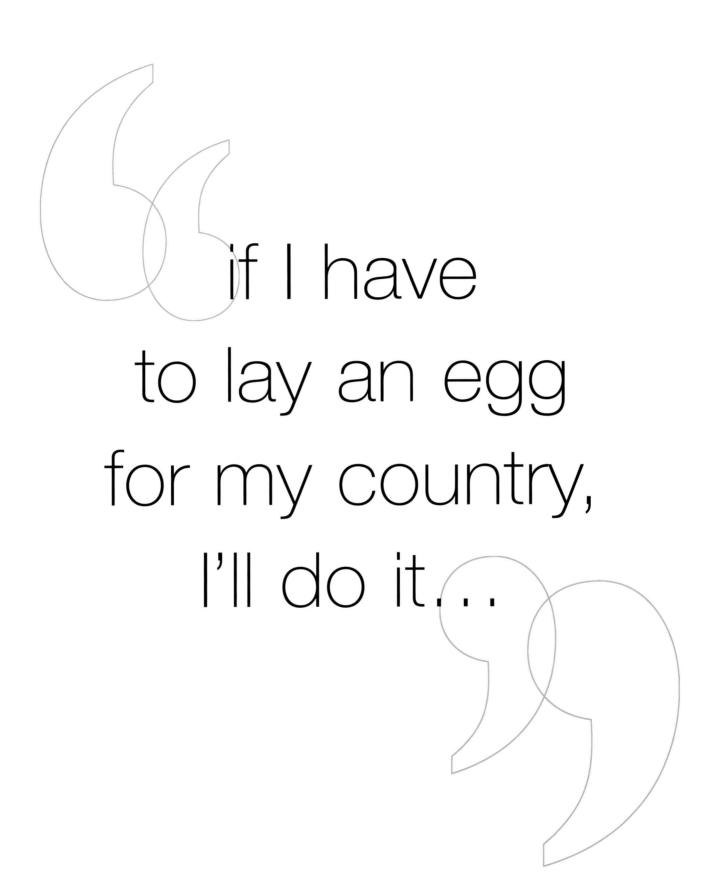

"if I have
to lay an egg
for my country,
I'll do it…"

heston blumenthal
quoting bob hope

THE FAT DUCK, BRAY, ENGLAND

smoked bacon-and-egg ice-cream
with French toast, morel mushrooms, salt butter toffee, tea aspic, tomato jelly, and a glass of mimosa

serves 4

syrup
3 ounces (85 g) superfine sugar
4 cups (1 l) mineral water
1 ¾ tablespoons lemon juice
½ teaspoon malic acid*
3 sachets of green tea
4 sachets of Earl Grey tea
2 sachets of Lapsang Souchong tea
1 sachet of Darjeeling tea
2 leaves softened gelatin

tea aspic
3 cups (750 ml) syrup
2 leaves softened gelatin

mimosa
1 cup freshly squeezed orange juice
1 cup champagne

smoked bacon-and-egg ice-cream
For four cups (1 l) of ice-cream:
10 ounces (300 g) maple smoked bacon
1 ¾ ounces (50 g) Alsace smoked
  slab bacon*
4 cups (1 l) milk
1 ¾ tablespoons skimmed
  milk powder
14 ounces (400 g) egg yolks
4 ½ ounces (125 g) liquid glucose

tomato jelly
2 ½ pounds (1.2 kg) ripe vine tomatoes
1 red pepper
scant 1 cup (100 g) confectioners' sugar
2 or 3 drops Worcester sauce
2 or 3 drops white wine vinegar
1 ½ tablespoons olive oil
3 coffee beans

salt butter toffee
scant 2 cups (375 g) superfine sugar
scant 2 cups (375 g) glucose
10 ½ ounces (300 g) salted butter
generous 1 ½ cups (350 ml) milk
scant 1 pint (450 ml) whipped cream

morel mushrooms
3 ½ ounces (100 g) dried morels
¾–1 cup (200 ml) Macvin du Jura*
½ cup (125 g) superfine sugar
½ cup (125 g) butter
1 ¾ tablespoons water

egg mix for the french toast
2 cups (500 ml) milk
4 tablespoons (50 g) superfine sugar
2 tablespoons La Vieille Noix
  hazelnut liqueur
3 ½ ounces (100 g) eggs

french toast
1 slice brioche
egg mix (see above)
7 tablespoons (100 g)
  clarified butter
6 tablespoons (75 g) superfine
  sugar

to finish the dish
maple syrup
17 fluid ounces (500 ml)
  liquid nitrogen
2 cups (500 ml) smoked
  bacon-and-egg ice-cream,
  prepared earlier (see above)

* see glossary, page 190

1 SYRUP
Dissolve the sugar in the mineral water and cool to 39°F (4°C) before adding the lemon juice and malic acid. Add the teabags and leave to infuse for twenty to thirty minutes. Strain through a fine strainer.

1 ASPIC
Heat a scant half cup (100 ml) of the syrup and add the gelatin, stirring all the time. Stir carefully to dissolve the gelatin thoroughly, then add the remaining syrup and mix in well. Strain through a fine strainer and leave overnight in the refrigerator.

1 MIMOSA DRINK
Pour the juice into a mixer or juice extractor so it foams up. Pour the champagne into four glasses. Pour the orange juice onto the champagne and divide the juice and foam evenly between the four glasses.

Preparation at the table of smoked bacon-and-egg ice-cream at the Fat Duck.

1 SMOKED BACON-AND-EGG ICE-CREAM

The day before serving, cook the bacon in the oven at 360° F (180°C) until it turns golden and chop it roughly. Mix with the milk and powdered milk and leave to infuse overnight.

2

The next day, beat the egg yolks with the glucose until the mixture whitens and doubles in volume (about ten minutes in an electric mixer). Pour the bacon and milk mixture into a large saucepan and heat until it begins to simmer, then add the egg and glucose mix, stirring continuously.

3

Pour everything into a saucepan and heat to 185°F (85°C). The high temperature is essential to coagulate the egg proteins and the aroma of scrambled eggs. Keep it at 185°F (85°C) for thirty seconds, then remove from the heat and cool as quickly as possible by pouring into a bowl set over ice. Strain to remove the bacon then blend to obtain a smooth cream before straining again. Store in the refrigerator.

TOMATO JELLY

Blanch, peel, and de-seed the tomatoes, then cut into tiny dice. Do likewise with the red pepper, cutting the dice even smaller than the tomato. Put all the ingredients in a wide, heavy-bottomed saucepan and cook at a very low heat for 2 ½ to 3 hours until you obtain a thick, sticky jelly. Remove the coffee beans, cool, and store in the refrigerator.

SALT BUTTER TOFFEE

Heat the sugar, glucose, butter, and milk in a pan. Cook over a moderate heat to 300°F (147°C), stirring constantly. Reduce the temperature and gently stir in the whipped cream. Cool and store in the refrigerator.

1 MOREL MUSHROOMS

Wash the mushrooms and get rid of any fine dirt. Mix with the other ingredients and cook over a low heat for ten to fifteen minutes until the morels soften.

2

Remove the mushrooms from the pan with a skimmer and reduce the cooking liquid until it becomes syrupy, then pour it over the mushrooms. Cool and store in the refrigerator.

1 EGG MIX FOR THE FRENCH TOAST

Beat all the ingredients together then strain in a fine sieve and store in the refrigerator.

1 MAKING THE FRENCH TOAST

Heat the oven to 300°F (150°C). Cut the slice of brioche into four rectangles 1 x 2 inches (2.5 x 5 cm) and put them in a shallow dish. Pour the egg mix over them and leave to soak for five minutes, turning them over every minute.

2

Melt the clarified butter and paint it on both sides of the brioche. Heat the brioche pieces in the oven.

3

Heat a nonstick skillet on a moderate heat and cook the sugar until it caramelizes. Add the slices of brioche and turn them over in the caramel until all sides are evenly coated with a fine layer of the sugar. Remove and arrange in the center of each plate.

TO FINISH AND SERVE

Make a little oval-shaped "quenelle" or ball with the salt butter toffee, using a spoon, and place it next to the French toast. Reheat the morels and position three on top of the toffee. On the other side of the French toast, place a spoon of tomato jelly, flattening the top to make a hollow that the ice-cream will sit on. Dribble a few drops of maple syrup on the plate using a pipette or the handle of a spoon.

MIXING THE ICE-CREAM AND NITROGEN

Have ready a wooden spoon, a bowl, a damp cloth, and the liquid nitrogen. Pour the bacon-and-egg cream into the bowl then slowly pour in the liquid nitrogen, stirring all the time. You may not need to use the full quantity of liquid nitrogen, so it is advisable not to pour it all in at the same time. The cream will begin to turn to ice-cream. Continue stirring until you obtain the texture of scrambled eggs. Position a ball of bacon-and-egg ice-cream on the tomato jelly and serve with the tea aspic.

SUGGESTED ACCOMPANIMENT MIMOSA COCKTAIL

jacques decoret
quoting thomas nurner
JACQUES DECORET, VICHY, FRANCE

"a hen
laid an egg,
the lord got
the yolk,
the lady the white
and the farmer,
the shell."

whole duck egg
with shell

1
Separate the whites from the yolks of the duck eggs.

2
Pre-heat the oven to 120° F (50° C). Wrap the yolks between two sheets of plastic wrap and place in the oven for thirty minutes.

3
Shape the softened butter into four eggs the same size and shape as the duck eggs.

4
Beat the two hen's eggs and dip the butter "eggs" in the beaten egg before dredging with the rice flour.

5
Quickly deep-fry at 392°F (200°C), then carefully remove the butter by cutting an aperture 1 ½ inches (4 cm) wide, as in the photograph.

6
Clean the bean shoots, grate the lime zest, and cut the red onion into matchsticks, and blanch in boiling water. Chop the spring onions finely, cut the ginger into julienne strips, and separate the pomegranate seeds. Set everything aside.

7
Quickly fry the bean shoots in the sesame seed oil. Sweat the spring onion without any oil and add the pomegranate molasses. Strain the sauce and thicken with a knob of butter.

8
Arrange the yolk inside the egg and the garnish in front of it. Season with the crushed pepper and Maldon sea salt.

9
Spoon a little of the pomegranate molasses sauce on each egg.

RECOMMENDED ACCOMPANIMENT SAKÉ KAMOSHIBITO KUHEIJI

serves 4

4 duck eggs
1 ½ cups (350g) softened butter
2 hen's eggs
1 pound (500 g) rice flour
vegetable oil, for deep-frying
1 ½ ounces (40 g) bean shoots
1 lime
¾ ounce (20 g) red onion
¾ ounce (20 g) spring onion
½ teaspoon ginger
1 tablespoon pomegranate seeds
2 ¾ tablespoons (35 ml) sesame oil
3 ½ tablespoons (50 ml)
  pomegranate molasses
1 tablespoon (30 g) butter
crushed black pepper
maldon sea salt

jacques dereux
quoting umberto eco (quoting samuel butler…)

JACQUES DEREUX, PARIS, FRANCE

"a hen is
only an
egg's way
of making
another
egg."

arroz nero (black rice)

1 THE DAY BEFORE

Make a stock from the ingredients listed.
Note that fish stock should not be cooked for more than 30 minutes after boiling.

2 THE RICE

The next day, in a heavy-bottomed saucepan, sweat the onion and garlic in the olive oil. When the vegetables have begun to turn a pale color, add the rice and stir well. The rice will turn translucent; add the white wine and leave to evaporate.

3

Cover with just enough stock, stirring all the time, and leave it to cook, adding more stock as necessary so it does not dry out. Cooking should take around fifteen minutes.

4

Cut the squid and the shrimp into tiny dice, mix with the squid ink and add to the rice. Add the cold butter in pieces and mix well. Bind the rice with the grated Parmesan.

5

Arrange the rice using a pastry ring on the dish. Place a hard-boiled egg yolk just off-center on the dish and remove a spoonful of rice from the center. Fill the cavity with the raw egg yolk.

RECOMMENDED WINE RED BURGUNDY, MERCUREY 1ᴱᴿ CRU, CLOS DES MYGLANDS 2001

serves 4

4 hard boiled eggs
4 egg yolks

stock
6 cups (1.5 l) water
2 cups (500 ml) dry white wine
1 onion
1 carrot
1 stick of celery
thyme
bay leaf
Italian parsley
1 clove garlic
1 leek
1 lemon
pepper
2 pounds (1 kg) fish bones and
    Dublin bay prawn carcasses

rice
1 chopped onion
1 clove garlic
olive oil
generous ½ pound (300g)
    canarolio or arborio rice
1 glass dry white wine
4 cups (1 l) stock
7 ounces (200 g) cooked squid
7 ounces (200 g) cooked shrimp
scant ½ cup (100 ml) squid ink
3 tablespoons (40 g) cold butter
4 teaspoons grated Parmesan
salt and pepper

"what's
in an egg?
E.G.G.
Exceptional,
Good,
Glorious."

softly-softly egg with *petit gris* snails buttered zucchini with parmesan, and peppermint

serves 4

4 eggs

diced zucchini
¼ pound (120 g) violin zucchini,
  chopped into tiny dice
1 ½ tablespoons olive oil
garlic clove
thyme
salt and pepper

julienne of zucchini
1 ½ ounces (40 g) violin zucchini,
  cut into julienne strips

soft-cooked tomatoes
4 whole tomatoes
1 ½ tablespoons olive oil
½ teaspoon sugar

beaten snail butter
scant ½ cup (100 ml) pale stock
½ cup (100 ml) stock made
  from cooking snails in
  a court-bouillon*
1 cup (250 g) unsalted butter

mint foam
generous ¾ cup (200 ml) milk
2 bunches peppermint
generous ¾ cup (200 ml)
  pouring cream
scant ½ cup (100 ml) pale stock
scant ½ cup (100 ml) stock
  made from cooking snails
  in a court bouillon
1 ¼ teaspoons agar-agar
2 teaspoons chlorophyll
  (see method)

chlorophyl
4 pounds (2 kg) spinach

serving and presentation
olive oil, for sautéeing
3 tablespoons (20 g)
  chopped snails
2 ½ tablespoons Parmesan
beaten snail butter
1 ½ tablespoons grilled pine nuts,
  roughly chopped
edible white flowers
2 teaspoons garlic oil

* see glossary, page 190

1 COOKING THE EGGS

Cook the eggs in water or in a steamer for twenty-five minutes at 150°F (64°C). Stop the cooking process by plunging them into cold water, then peel them.

2 DICED ZUCCHINI

Sweat the diced zucchini in the olive oil with the garlic clove and a sprig of thyme, season, then cool quickly. Set aside.

3 JULIENNE OF ZUCCHINI

Cook the julienne of zucchini in boiling water, drain and refresh in cold water. Set aside.

4 SOFT-COOKED TOMATOES

Peel, de-seed, and cut the tomatoes in quarters. Arrange them on a sheet of silicone paper, drizzle with olive oil, and sprinkle with sugar. Cook in a 122°F (50°C) oven for eight hours.

5 BEATEN SNAIL BUTTER

Bring a scant ½ cup (100 ml) of pale stock to the boil and the same quantity of snail flavored stock. Using a blender, incorporate the very cold butter in pieces and blend thoroughly.

6 PREPARING THE MINT FOAM

For the mint-flavored milk, bring the milk to the boil and infuse two bunches of peppermint for twelve hours, for two of which the milk should be warm. Store in the refrigerator and strain before using.

7 PREPARING THE CHLOROPHYLL

Blend the spinach with cold water and strain the resulting mixture through a muslin cloth, pressing hard to extract as much juice as possible. Bring to the boil and skim off the foam, which is all you need to keep, and cool it rapidly.

8 FINISHING THE MINT FOAM

Bring the mint-flavored milk to the boil with the cream, ½ cup (100 ml) pale stock, the snail-flavored bouillon, and the agar-agar, then incorporate the chlorophyll. Cool quickly so that it keeps its green color.

9 SERVING AND PRESENTATION

In a heavy skillet or sauté pan, heat a little olive oil and sauté the snails. Add the diced zucchini, the soft-cooked tomatoes, and the Parmesan. Thicken it with a little of the snail butter. Strain in a fine sieve and spread it on the bottom of the serving dish, then sprinkle with the grilled pine nuts.

In another pan, sweat the julienne of zucchini with a little garlic oil. Thicken with a spoon of snail butter. Drain and dribble it around the snail stuffing.

Arrange the egg on top, sprinkle with Parmesan and add all the snails and the mint foam around it. Edible white flowers, and a julienne of tomatoes also make a suitable garnish for this dish.

RECOMMENDED WINE SAINT PÉRAY, PIC CHAPOUTIER, 2004

vanina villarreal
quoting a Galician proverb

LE FOGON, PARIS

"better an egg offered as a gift than an egg eaten alone.

caramel flan

serves 6

25 egg yolks
1 whole egg
8 cups (2 l) milk
1 pound (500g) superfine sugar
1 stick cinnamon
zest of 1 lemon
1 vanilla pod

to caramelize the flan mold
generous ½ cup (125 g)
  superfine sugar
scant 2 tablespoons salted butter
scant ½ cup (100 ml) pouring cream

1
Heat the milk in a saucepan together with the
sugar, cinnamon, lemon zest, and vanilla. Reduce
by one-quarter and leave to cool.

2
In a large bowl beat the egg yolks and whole egg
and add the flavored milk.

3 CARAMELIZING THE FLAN MOLD
Heat the cream in a saucepan. In a second pan,
caramelize the sugar over moderate heat, without
adding anything else. Add the butter and cream and
bring to the boil before pouring into a large mold.

4
Pour in the egg mixture and bake for fifty minutes
at 300°F (150°C). When cooked, unmold onto
a serving dish.

RECOMMENDED WINE VIN À L'ORANGE,
IGLESIAS DE HUELVA CELLARS

*You can also make this flan in individual molds as
shown in the photograph.*

nathalie robert
quoting edmond rostand

LE PAIN DE SUCRE, PARIS, FRANCE

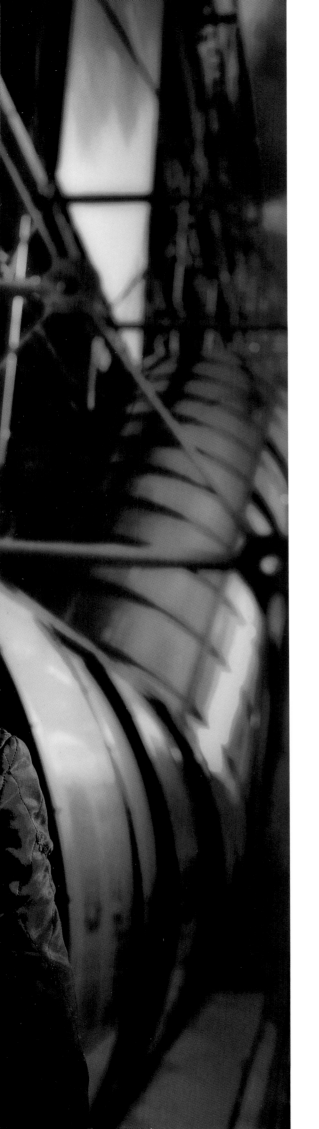

an egg looks as though it might be made of marble, until it breaks.

kadaïf shell
**1 ½ tablespoons butter
¾ tablespoon honey,
  chestnut-flavored if possible
¾ ounce (10 g) fresh Kadaïf*
  (angel-hair pasta)**

saffron yolks
**3 egg yolks
½–¾ cup (120–150 ml) milk
1 pinch saffron
1 tablespoon sugar
pinch fine salt
½ teaspoon gelatin**

pistachio sponge
**2 egg whites
3 tablespoons (40 g) superfine
  sugar
1 ½ tablespoons flour
⅓ cup (25 g) ground almonds
1 ½ tablespoons chopped
  pistachios**

espelette pepper cream
**½ cup (125 ml) milk
1 ¾ tablespoons flour
2 tablespoons egg yolk
1 tablespoon superfine sugar
1 pinch espelette pepper***

safrron and espelette
pepper duo

1 KADAÏF PASTRY CASE
Clarify the butter and mix with the honey, preferably a chestnut-flavored variety. Baste the Kadaïf with this mixture and use it to line 4 two-inch (5 cm) hemispherical molds. Cook for ten minutes at 320°F (160°C).

2 SAFFRON CREAM
Infuse the saffron in the milk and make a custard using the yolks, the sugar, and salt. Cook it for five minutes on a very gentle heat. Add the gelatin and pour into eight smaller hemispherical molds. Freeze and unmold.

3 PISTACHIO SPONGE
Beat the egg whites to stiff peaks and add the sugar. Fold in the flour and ground almonds. Spread the mixture on a baking sheet, sprinkle with the chopped pistachios, and bake at 320°F (160°C) for ten minutes. Cut a series of little circles from the sponge.

4 ESPELETTE PEPPER CREAM
Bring all the ingredients to the boil and cook, as for a pastry cream. Place the sponge disc on the saffron cream and add the Espelette pepper cream. Sandwich together. Place each in a Kadaïf shell.

SUGGESTED ACCOMPANIMENT FRESH GREEN TEA

* see glossary, page 190

"if the world is an egg, then the earth is its yolk."

carlo cracco
quoting chad heng
CRACCO-PECK, MILAN, ITALY

salad of crispy

serves 4

for the green leaves
3 egg whites
1 ounce (30 g) fresh spinach,
   puréed
salt

for the yellow leaves
3 egg whites
1 sachet saffron
salt

for the black leaves
3 egg whites
3 ½ tablespoons (50 ml) squid ink
salt

for the white leaves
3 egg whites
salt

for the red leaves
3 egg whites
1 teaspoon paprika

to serve
chicory
extra virgin oil
watercress

1
Using an electric mixer, beat each set of egg whites separately into stiff peaks. Add each ingredient for color, and season with salt.

2
In a nonstick skillet, melt a knob of butter and, using a brush, spread a little of each mixture on the hot pan. Cook for 15 seconds.

3
Remove and leave each leaf to dry.

4
In a transparent bowl, place a leaf of each color. Cover with finely sliced chicory and season with the extra virgin olive oil and salt.

5
Decorate with a few red and green watercress leaves before serving.

RECOMMENDED WINE
GEWURTZTRAMINER 2002

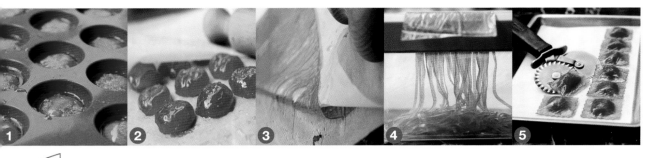

egg spaghetti with garlic, oil, and chilli pepper

serves 4

generous ½ pound (300 g)
  cooked egg spaghetti
  (see opposite)
1 ½ tablespoons milk
1 ½ heads garlic
olive oil
ground chilli pepper
20 leaves deep-fried Italian parsley

1
Boil the milk and garlic and reduce by half.

2
Strain through a fine sieve and set aside.

3
In a skillet, heat a little oil and add the cooked spaghetti and a little chilli pepper. Sauté for two minutes and serve in a deep dish.

4
Sprinkle with deep-fried parsley and drizzle a dash of oil over the top.

RECOMMENDED WINE
CASTELLO DI BROLIO 2000, CHIANTI CLASSICO

YOLK BASE, FOR PASTA

6 egg yolks
2 pounds (1 kg) smoked salt
½ pound (250 g) sugar
½ pound (250 g) red bean purée

1

Mix the salt, sugar, and red bean purée. Place a spoonful of this mixture at the bottom of an individual mold and cover it with an egg yolk, then cover with another tablespoon of the mixture.

2

Leave to marinate for four hours at room temperature, turning the molds over after two hours so that the marinating occurs uniformly.

3

At the end of four hours, wash the yolks under running water for ten seconds and reserve on a plate. The yoke pasta base is now ready **(1)**.

BASIC PASTA

12 marinated, dried egg yolks
2 sheets silicone paper
oil, for greasing

1

Oil the paper and lay the egg yolks on it **(2)**.

2

Cover with the other sheet of silicone paper, then roll it with a rolling pin to create a thin sheet **(3)**.

3

Leave to dry for four or five hours at room temperature. The basic pasta is now ready.

THREE RECIPES USING BASIC EGG PASTA

1 SPAGHETTI
Cut the egg pasta into regular-sized squares.

2
Cut into spaghetti using the blade of a pasta machine **(4)**.

1 GRATED EGG YOLKS
Keep the egg yolks at room temperature for five or six days or until they are completely dried out. Grate them onto pasta or a salad.

EGG RAVIOLI WITH MEAT FILLING

4 ounces (100 g) minced beef
4 teaspoons mustard
fine salt and white pepper

1

Spread a little of the stuffing on the egg pasta.

2

Cover with another layer of pasta.

3

Cut ½ inch (1 cm) square raviolis using a fluted cutter **(5)**.

the best friendships always have a little emptiness in them, just like an egg.

michel roux jr.
quoting jules renard

LE GAVROCHE, LONDON

soufflé suissesse

1

Pre-heat the oven to 400° F (200°C).

2

Melt the butter in a heavy-bottomed saucepan, add the flour and stir for around a minute. Pour in the milk and boil for around three minutes, stirring all the time so that no lumps form.

3

Add the egg yolks and remove from the heat. Season with the salt and pepper. Cover with greased silicone paper, to prevent a skin from forming.

4

Beat the whites into stiff peaks (but do not beat them too much). Add ⅓ of the whites to the milk mixture and stir in using an electric beater, then fold in the remaining whites carefully.

5

Butter individual tartlet molds 3 inches (8 cm) in diameter and divide the soufflé mixture among them. Bake in the oven for three minutes until the surface begins to brown. As they are cooking, season the cream and heat it gently. Pour into a gratin dish.

6

Unmold the soufflés onto the cream. Sprinkle with the grated cheese and return to the oven for a further five minutes. Serve at once.

RECOMMENDED WINE RIESLING 2002, BRAND ZIND-HUMBRECHT

serves 4

5 egg yolks
6 egg whites
butter
3 tablespoons (45 g) flour
2 cups (500 ml) milk
2 ½ cups (550 ml) heavy cream
salt and freshly ground white pepper
scant ½ pound (200 g) grated
  emmental or Gruyère cheese

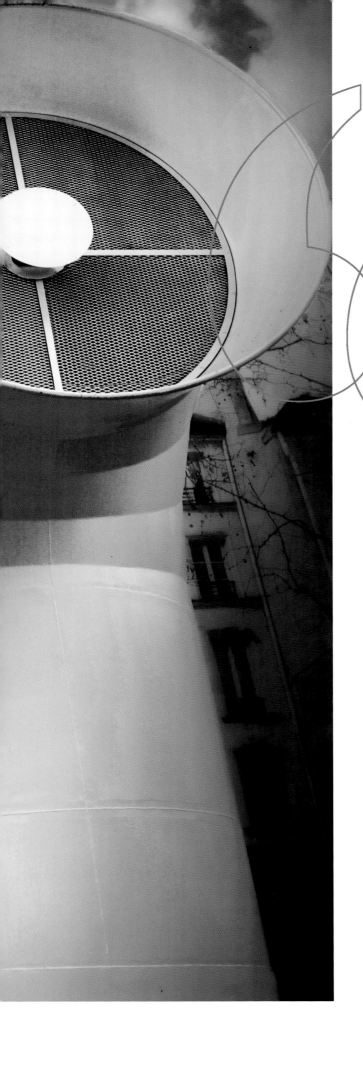

didier mathray
quoting an ancient Greek proverb
LE PAIN DE SUCRE, PARIS

"better an egg this year than a hen the next."

serves 4

meringue
½ cup (125 g) egg white
1 combawa (a citrus fruit
   from Thailand), or a lemon,
   a lime, or a yuzu
scant 4 ounces (120 g)
   superfine sugar
2 cups (100 g) confectioners'
   sugar

marshmallow
generous ½ cup (150 g)
   egg white
6 generous cups (1.5 l) water
½ pound (500 g) sugar
1 cup (200 g) glucose
2 tablespoons superfine sugar
¾–1 ounce (25 g) gelatin leaves
2 tablespoons orange
   flower water
⅓ cup (70 g) blackcurrant coulis
2 tablespoons cocoa powder
½ cup (50 g) roughly chopped
   bitter chocolate

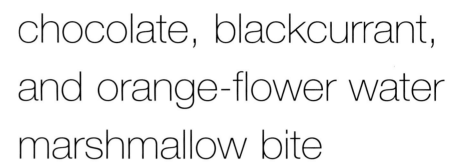

chocolate, blackcurrant, and orange-flower water marshmallow bite

1 MERINGUE
Grate the zests of the combawa or other citrus fruit and squeeze the juice. Beat the egg whites into soft peaks, then mix in the superfine sugar and the fruit juice. Continue beating the egg whites and delicately incorporate the confectioners' sugar and the grated fruit zest. Spread a thin layer of this meringue on two oiled baking sheets. Cook for 1 ½ hours at 250°F (120°C), then leave to dry for a further 1 ½ hours at 210°F (100°C).

2 MARSHMALLOW
Prepare a syrup with the water, the sugar, and the glucose. Cook to 266°F (130°C). When the thermometer shows 255°F (125°C), start beating the egg whites and make a classic meringue by adding the two tablespoons of sugar. Pour the boiling syrup onto the egg whites, beating all the time.

3
Soften the gelatin leaves in a little water and dissolve them in the marshmallow meringue. Divide the mixture into three bowls. Flavor the first with the orange-flower water, the second with the blackcurrant coulis and the last with the cocoa and chopped bitter chocolate.

4
Pour each bowl of marshmallow onto a separate sheet of silicone paper in a lightly oiled frame or cake pan. Leave to cool and remove the frame.

5
Cut six pieces of meringue the same size as the marshmallow. Sandwich the marshmallow between each slab of meringue. Using a serrated edged knife, cut each slab into bite-size pieces.

SUGGESTED ACCOMPANIMENT YOGHURT MILKSHAKE OR SWEETENED INDIAN LASSI

egg

Gulls' eggs

notes

restaurant addresses

further reading

ALI-BAB. *The Encyclopedia of Practical Gastronomy*, New York: McGraw-Hill, 1974

HESTON BLUMENTHAL. *Family Food: A New Approch to Cooking*, New York: Penguin Global, 2006

TERRENCE AND VICKI CONRAN. *Classic Conran: Plain, Simple and Satisfying Food*, London: Conran Octopus, 2006

MADELEINE PELNER COSMAN. *Fabulous Feasts: Midieval Cookery and Ceremony*, New York: George Braziller, 2003

FATÉMA HAL. *The Food of Morocco: Authentic Recipes from the North African Coast*, London: Periplus Publishing, 2003

PIERRE HERMÉ AND DORIE GREENSPAN. *Desserts by Pierre Hermé*, New York: Little, Brown, 1998

LOUISA JONES, JACQUES CHIBOIS, AND DAN BARBER. *Provence Harvest*, New York: Stewart, Tabori and Chang, 2005

THOMAS KELLER. *Bouchon*, New York: Artisan, 2004

GILLES PUDLOWSKI AND MAURICE ROUGEMOUNT. *Great Women Chefs of Europe*, Paris: Flammarion, 2005

MICHEL ROUX JR. *Matching Food and Wine: Classic and Not So Classic Combinations*, London: Weidenfeld & Nicholson, 2005

MICHEL ROUX AND MARTIN BRIGDALE. *Eggs*, Hoboken: John Wiley, 2006

ÉRIC RIPERT AND MICHAEL RHULMAN. *A Return to Cooking*, New York: Artisan, 2002

REAY TANNAHILL. *Food in History*, New York: Three Rivers Press, 1995

HERVÉ THIS. *Molecular Gastronomy: Exploring the Science of Flavor*, New York: Columbia University Press, 2005

glossary

AGAR-AGAR: seaweed, based gelling agent

ALSACE SMOKED SLAB BACON: A very highly smoked bacon with an almost black rind.

BLANCH: Method of boiling for a short time certain meats and vegetables as a means of pre-cooking them.

CLARIFY: To remove impurities present in a liquid by filtering or with the aid of egg white.

COURT BOUILLON: A seasoned liquid usually made from water and vegetables, (carrot, onion, celery, leek), and sometimes with white wine or lemon juice added. It is cooked for only a short time and often used for poaching fish or other delicately flavored foods.

ESPELETTE PEPPER: Type of jalapeno pepper from the Basque region of France that can be eaten fresh but is usually made into a wide variety of condiments or, most commonly, hung in bunches and dried. It has a distinct smokey-spicey flavour, but other ground chilli powder can be used instead.

FLEUR DE SEL: A sea salt with a distinct flavor. It is hand harvested and taken from the first layer of the salt bed. Other sea salts or kosher salt make subsititutes.

GASTRIQUE: Orange or raspberry sauce that usually involves a sweet/sour combination.

INVERTED SUGAR SYRUP: A sucrose-based syrup that is sweeter than ordinary sugar (which means less can be used). It is commercially available ready-made.

ISO-MALT: Artificial sugar substitute that is 0.45 times as sweet as ordinary sugar (Sucrosed-based).

KADAÏF: Fresh pasta vermicelli made from soft flour. It originated in Greece and Turkey and is also known as angel-hair pasta.

MACVIN DU JURA: A fortified wine from the Jura region.

MALIC ACID: naturally occuring bicarboxylic acid found in apples, pears and grape juice

PALE STOCK: Stock made from veal bones, chicken trimmings, and offal with carrots, celery, and onions.

SIPHON: Kitchen implement used for making fruit or vegetable mousses.

WASABI: Type of horseradish root originally from the cabbage family, used as a condiment, particularly in Japanese cookery.

egg suppliers

United Kingdom

BRE-PEN FARM SHOP
Mawgan Porth
Newquay
Cornwall, TR8 4AL
tel.: 01637860420
http://www.bre-penfarm.co.uk/shop.html
Farm sales every day in winter from
10.00 am—5.30 pm and in summer from
10.00 am—6.00 pm

CROCKFORD BRIDGE FARM
New Haw Road
Addlestone, KT15 2BU
tel.: 01932852630
www.crockfordbridgefarm.co.uk
info@crockfordbridgefarm.co.uk
A large range of fresh produce, including chicken, eggs, cheese,
pickles, chutney, and honey.
Farm sales every day from
9.00 am—5.30 pm, Monday—Wednesday
9.00 am—6.00 pm, Thursday—Saturday
10.00 am—4.30 pm Sunday

United States

J-14 Agriculutrual Enterprises/ Camp C.A.R.V.E.R.
4600 Sortor Drive
Kansas City, KS 66104
http://www.localharvest.org/farms/M13578

DREAMFARM
Cross Plains, WI, 53528
tel.: (608) 767-3442
http://www.dreamfarm.biz/default.htm

WINGSHADOWS HACIENDA
39451 Hightway 79
Warner Springs CA, 92086
tel.: (951) 767-2710
wingshadowsranch@aol.com
www.geocities.com/wwmicasa1/Wingshadows.html

ALEXIS FREE RANGE EGGS
Lebanon, CT
tel.: (860) 690-7593
WildBittersweet2@aol.com

BEE HEAVEN FARM
Redland, Florida
tel.: (270) 536-3034
http://www.redlandorganics.com

KEEP ON CLUCKIN'
1434 Idaho Rd.
Williamsburg, KS 66095
tel.: (785) 746-5433
keeponcluckin@yahoo.com

DIXIE CHIKS RANCH
Custer, Kentucky
tel.: (270) 536-3034
Dixie_Chiks_Ranch@yahoo.com
http://www.freewebs.com/dixiechiks/

FARMER'S KITCHEN
275 Highway 504
Natchitoches, LA 71457
tel.: (318) 354-7353 or (318) 663-7355
poultryfarmer001@aol.com

FARM FRESH ORGANICS
Hamilton, Montana
tel.: (406) 375-9187
prlponderosa@msn.com

THE LITTLE BLACK HEN
4367 St., Rt. 29 E.
Sidney, Ohio 45365
littleblackhen@earthlink.net